READY for RICA™

A Test Preparation Guide for California's Reading Instruction Competence Assessment

James J. Zarrillo

California State University, Hayward

Merrill
Prentice Hall

Upper Saddle River, New Jersey
Columbus, Ohio

Vice President and Publisher: Jeffery W. Johnston
Editor: Linda Ashe Montgomery
Production Editor: JoEllen Gohr
Cover Designer: Diane C. Lorenzo
Cover art: Photo Disc
Production Manager: Pamela Bennett
Director of Marketing: Kevin Flanagan
Marketing Manager: Krista Groshong
Marketing Services Manager: Barbara Koontz

10 9 8 7 6 5 4 3 2 1

ISBN: 0-13-041295-3

Table of Contents

Introduction:
The Test and Test-Taking Strategies

If you have purchased this book, you probably are enrolled in a Multiple Subject Credential Program in California. In addition to completing your courses and field experience, you must pass the Reading Instruction Competence Assessment (RICA) to earn your credential. The purpose of this book is to help you pass the RICA. There are two formats for the RICA, a written test and video performance assessment. This book will prepare you to take the written examination.

There are a few considerations you should keep in mind while you study from this book. It was written for credential candidates who have taken (or who are taking) reading methods courses. This book is not a substitute for coursework or a more comprehensive methodology text on how to teach reading. This book is meant to be read as a review for RICA. It is "streamlined," containing the essential information you should know before you take the test. You can find out more about the topics covered in this book, including references to journal articles and books, in your reading methods textbook. My purpose is not to analyze elementary reading instruction; my purpose is to help you pass the RICA.

The RICA is a "high stakes, exit exam." The good news is that *with proper preparation* the chances are very good that you will pass the test. From June of 1998 to June of 1999, over 14,000 people took the written form of the RICA. Ninety percent passed the exam. Please don't let this high passing rate fool you. The RICA is a difficult test and the high passage rate no doubt reflects the hard work of the people who took it. In this introductory chapter, I will discuss the test itself and some test-taking strategies that will help you to be successful.

An Overview of The Test

There are three parts to the RICA:

* Multiple Choice Questions

* Focused Educational Problems and Instructional Tasks

* A Case Study

Let's take a closer look at each section.

Multiple Choice Questions

The RICA includes 70 multiple choice questions. Ten of the questions are "experimental," and are being tested for future RICAs. You will not know which ten are experimental, so you must try to get every question correct.

Focused Educational Problems and Instructional Tasks

You will have four essay questions to answer. Two of the questions will require a short answer. The *RICA™ Registration Bulletin* suggests an answer of only 50 words for the two short essays. The other two questions will require a longer answer. The *RICA Registration Bulletin* suggests answers of 150 words.

The Case Study

The case study is another essay question. You will be presented with test data about a student and challenged to describe instructional strategies that will help the student become a better reader. The *RICA Registration Bulletin* suggests an answer of 300 words.

Test-Taking Strategies for the RICA

(1) Don't Waste Time "Self-Assessing" Because You Don't Have to Get Every Answer Right to Pass the Test

One advantage you have with the RICA is that you don't have to answer every question right to pass the test. There are 120 points possible on the test. A score of 81 is passing. That is 67.5%!!! So, the following two thoughts should not enter your head: "Hey, I'm doing great on this test," or "Oh my gosh, I'm going to fail." <u>Don't waste your time evaluating your performance</u>. Your attitude when you take the test should be very business-like. Just answer the questions.

(2) Budget Your Time

On most timed, "high stress" tests like the RICA, the most common reason people fail is NOT a lack of knowledge. Rather it is from not budgeting the time you spend on each question. The more questions you answer the better your chances for passing the test. Here is more good news about the RICA. You have four hours to complete the test, and you can spend the time however you want. I recommend the following:

Multiple Choice Section: 90 minutes

Short Essays: 30 minutes (15 minutes each)

Long Essays: 50 minutes (25 minutes each)

Case Study: 60 minutes

<u>So, be sure you have a watch when you take the RICA and budget your time. If you follow my time guidelines, you will have ten extra minutes to use however you wish.</u>

(3) Develop a Strategy for Completing the Multiple Choice Section

I am of the opinion that on most tests like the RICA, the multiple choice questions are more difficult than the essay questions. So, don't get bogged down or frustrated on the multiple choice section of the RICA. Expect difficult questions. <u>The biggest mistake you can make, when completing the RICA multiple choice section, is to spend too much time on this section of the test.</u>

Answer every question; there is no penalty for guessing.

All multiple choice questions have two parts: (1) a "stem," which is a phrase, a sentence, or a paragraph which leads to the (2) "options." On the National Evaluation Systems (NES) RICA web site there are 14 sample multiple choice questions. Once again, NES is the company that developed and administers the RICA. Their web site is **http://www.rica.nesinc.com**. Click on "Written Examination;" the sample questions are links at the bottom of that section. If these sample questions are like the ones on the RICA, they will be fairly difficult to answer. *The "stems" of the questions are very long.* In fact, one sample question had a stem that was 70 words! You are probably used to multiple choice questions with short stems (i.e., "One strategy a fourth grade teacher could use to build reading comprehension is:"). Long stems make for complicated questions.

The *Registration Bulletin* says there will be two types of multiple choice questions. Some will be "content questions," which will ask if you know the content of RICA (i.e., "All informal reading inventories will include the following tests:"). The more difficult questions are of the second type; they will provide a classroom scenario and ask you to analyze a specific problem (i.e., "Teacher A has a second grade classroom with 20 students. She has assessed her students' knowledge of letter-sound relationships and determined that six of her students do not know the *ph* digraph makes the sound of */f/*. She should:").

To conclude, answer every question. Don't take more than 90 minutes on this section. Expect some difficult questions with long stems.

(4) Develop an Appropriate Strategy for Answering the Essays

There are two short essay questions. The essay questions are called *"Focused Educational Problems and Instructional Tasks."* Your answers should be between 50 and 100 words. Take about 15 minutes for each of these questions. There are two long essay questions. Your answers for the long questions should be between 150 and 250 words. Take about 25 minutes for each of the long questions.

All the essay questions present a hypothetical situation. You will get information about an entire class, a group of children, or an individual student. You must decide what an appropriate instructional intervention would be.

Be sure to take a look at the sample essay questions on the NES web site (**http://www.rica.nesinc.com**). Here are some things to remember when you write your answers:

* Answer what they ask, and come directly to the point. The people grading your essays will have lots of papers to read, so don't try to "snow" them.

* Write legibly. Don't expect the person reading your essays to read your essay over and over again to try to figure out what you wrote.

* Your answer should solve the challenge the question presents by:

<u>Identifying</u> appropriate instructional strategies,

<u>Providing</u> specific information about the strategy as it applies to the question, and

<u>Explaining</u> why the strategy will work.

Once again: Identify, provide specific information, explain.

* The sample test at the end of this book has two short essay and two long essay questions, just like the real RICA. The answer section provides examples of good responses to the essays.

(5) Plan Ahead to Use an Appropriate Strategy for Addressing the Case Study

The case study is worth 24 points, one-fifth of the total (120). You will be given "raw" assessment data for an individual student. The data you are provided may include the results of a reading interest survey, the teacher's copy of a miscue analysis of a student's oral reading, the results of the student reading lists of words, and other types of tests. I will review kinds of tests you need to know in subsequent chapters of this book.

The case study on the NES web site asks for an answer of three parts:

<u>First</u>, identify the student's <u>strengths</u> as a reader. Be sure to cite specific examples from the case study data to support your conclusions.

<u>Second</u>, identify the student's <u>areas of need</u>. Again, be sure to cite specific examples from the case study to support your conclusions.

<u>Finally</u>, identify an instructional <u>intervention to address each area of need</u>. Describe the intervention (types of lessons) and provide an example of one lesson. Explain how the intervention will help the student.

Once again, when answering the case study, tell about the student's strengths, areas of need, and interventions to address each area of need.

My advice on the case study is the same as for the essays. Come directly to the point and write legibly. The sample test at the end of this book has a case study and the answer section has an example of what your answer should look like.

(6) Recognize the Attitude of the Test Developers

When you take the RICA, you should adopt the attitude of the policy makers who created it: You believe in a "balanced" approach to reading instruction. As you might know, the field of reading instruction has zealous proponents of radically different approaches to teaching reading. The people who designed RICA believe that teachers should have a balanced instructional program with:

* The direct, explicit teaching of reading skills and strategies. A reading <u>skill</u> is something a reader does automatically. For example, a skillful reader knows that in the word *city*, the *c* makes an /s/ sound. A reading <u>strategy</u> is something a reader chooses to do, like reread a paragraph to clarify meaning. "Direct, explicit" teaching means that the teacher sets the objective for a lesson and teaches it in a pleasant, but no-nonsense manner.

* Opportunities to use the skills and strategies through meaningful reading and writing experiences, like reading library books and writing stories.

When you write your answers to the RICA, do not appear to be "unbalanced." That is, an overly zealous supporter of either side of the instructional spectrum. You believe that teachers should directly teach students the skills and strategies they need to be good readers. And, you believe students should spend a great deal of time reading and writing.

(7) Devote More Study Time to the Content Areas Which Are Emphasized

The Content Specifications for RICA define 13 content areas you must know (this book has a chapter on each content area). The 13 content areas, however, do not have equal weight on the test. Both the multiple choice questions and the essays emphasize the following eight content areas:

Content Area 3: Phonemic Awareness

Content Area 4: Concepts About Print

Content Area 5: Systematic, Explicit Phonics and Other Word Identification Strategies

Content Area 6: Spelling Instruction

Content Area 7: Reading Comprehension

Content Area 8: Literary Response and Analysis

Content Area 9: Content-Area Literacy

Content Area 10: Student Independent Reading

There will be questions on material from each of the 13 content areas. <u>It would be wise, however, to devote more time to the eight areas listed above than to the other five.</u>

(8) Read the Content Specifications. Check the NES RICA Web Site.

Be sure that you have read the Content Specifications for the RICA. They can be found in the *Registration Bulletin*. The Content Specifications are a detailed outline of what you must know. Look at the sample questions on the NES web site **http://www.rica.nesinc.com**. The questions on the NES web site are written in the same format as the questions you will answer on the test.

The California Commission on Teacher Credentialing (CCTC) is responsible for the RICA. For information on the test, click on their web site at **http://www.ctc.gov**.

The *Registration Bulletin* for the RICA is full of important information. It includes the content specifications for the exam. For a copy, call National Evaluation Systems (NES), the company who developed and administers the RICA, at 916-928-4004. The NES web site for RICA is **http://www.rica.nesinc.com**.

Chapter 1
Content Area 1:
Conducting Ongoing Assessment of Reading Development

Introduction

We continue now with a look at each of the 13 Content Areas of the RICA. The first Content Area establishes principles for the assessment of reading development. Assessment is the process of gathering, interpreting, and using data. The assessment of reading development is complicated because there are so many aspects of reading that must be measured. It is worth noting that the Content Specifications use the broader word "assessment," rather than "testing." While many aspects of reading development can be measured by tests, there are other ways of gathering information.

In this chapter, we are concerned with the general principles of assessment, some terminology you should know, and informal reading inventories (IRIs). The second Content Area covers how you plan, organize, and manage instruction. You will read about specific assessment instruments and procedures for each of the other 11 Content Areas in chapters 3–13.

Here are the three key points to remember about the assessment of reading development:

(1) Assessment Is Ongoing

Teachers should gather information about their students' reading performance throughout the school year. Most elementary school teachers have always done this, to some degree. On the other hand, in many classrooms, especially in high school and college, data is collected only at certain points of time, usually right before grades are due. The point the creators of RICA want to make is that valuable information is generated every day in classrooms. This is not to say, of course, that a teacher should collect information about every student, every day.

(2) Assessment Is a Process That Uses Multiple Sources

Subsequent chapters of this book will describe several ways of assessing student reading development. Some of them will be <u>formal</u> – tests of some sort. Others will be <u>informal</u> – such as collecting written work students complete, writing notes about students on a computer, or tape recording a discussion.

The point here is that teachers should <u>not</u> rely on <u>one</u> source of data to make judgments. For example, if you want to draw conclusions about a student's reading comprehension, you would (a) administer the reading passages from an IRI and ask literal comprehension questions, (b) use a CLOZE test to measure her ability to read content material, like a social studies textbook, (c) take notes on the student's performance during a discussion of a juvenile novel she had read, and (d) collect her written answers to inferential and evaluative questions you asked after she read a story from the basal reader.

(3) Assessment Drives Instruction

After a teacher collects information from a variety of sources and analyzes it to determine a student's strengths or weaknesses, the teacher should use this knowledge to plan instruction. In the ideal classroom, all instructional decisions would be based on the results of thorough assessment. Otherwise, teachers inevitably end up teaching some students skills and strategies they already know and teaching others skills and strategies that they cannot possibly learn because they do not have the prior knowledge to be successful or are not developmentally ready.

Assessment will determine how you group your students. Most of your groups will exist for a short time and will unite children who share a common need. For example, a kindergarten teacher has assessed her students' knowledge of concepts about print and determined that Joe, Lois, Leticia, and Thuy don't seem to understand the directionality of English (left to right, top to bottom). Those four students would meet with the teacher as a group to receive direct instruction on directionality.

Assessment will also determine the resources you use, the teaching strategies you select, and the pace at which you teach.

Basic Concepts and Terms

Reliability. A test is reliable if the results of the test yield consistent scores across administrations. In other words, if you were to take Form A of a test on April 1 and Form B on April 2, your scores would be considered reliable if they are almost identical.

Validity. A test is valid if it measures what it claims to measure. Let's take a moment to think further about this testing concept. Validity is a significant issue in the assessment of reading development. You might think that all scores on reading tests, developed by professional test makers, are valid. You might think that these scores always give you an accurate picture of what your students can and cannot do. This is not the case. Consider the assessment of reading comprehension. Students are scored on the comprehension knowledge they can provide after reading a text selection. For some students, these scores could be invalid because students possess the background knowledge to answer the questions at the end of a selection without reading it. For example, on a timed test, students read a three-paragraph selection on ancient Egypt. The first question asked, "Why did the ancient Egyptians build pyramids?" If these students had studied ancient Egypt during the school year, they might be able to answer the question even if they had not read the selection! Also, many reading comprehension tests developed long ago present reading selections that do not resemble the type of texts young children normally read now. Almost all stories our first graders read, for example, are illustrated. Until a few years ago, however, virtually all reading comprehension tests administered to first graders did not include stories with illustrations.

Standardized. A standardized test is one that has an established, non-varying procedure. Standardized tests have a manual for the person who administers the test, a script for the person to read. The tests have strict instructions and time limits. You have taken many tests like this – the person administering the test reads aloud something like, "Open your test booklet to page 5. Read the instructions silently. Begin working when I say 'start.' Continue until you reach the last item on page 12. Do not go on to page 13. You have 43 minutes. Start." The RICA, by the way, is a standardized test.

Norm-referenced. Norm-referenced scores allow for comparisons between the students taking the tests and a national average. The makers of commercially published reading tests, like the Stanford Achievement Tests (SAT) or the Comprehensive Tests of Basic Skills (CTBS) administer versions of the test to a sample of children. The result of this sample is used to create "norms," which are comparison scores. For example, a fourth grader taking a reading comprehension test gets 42 out of 60 questions correct; 42 is his "raw score." Is this good? Without norm-referenced scores you wouldn't know. If the average fourth grader in the sampling group scored 33, then our fourth grader scored above the average. He might well have a percentile score of 78 and a grade level equivalent score of 6.3. Both tell us that he was reading above the national norm.

Percentile Scores. Percentile scores are norm-referenced scores. Staying with our example, a fourth grader who has a percentile score of 78 had a higher raw score than 78% of the sampling group. The higher the percentile score the better. An "average" score would be 50. Someone with a percentile score of 15 has done poorly on the test, achieving a score higher than only 15% of the sampling group.

Grade Equivalent Scores. Grade equivalent scores are norm-referenced. A student's raw score is converted to a school grade level. Again, our fourth grader got 42 of 60 questions correct (his raw score). His percentile score probably would be around 78. It depends, of course, on how well the children in the sampling group did. His raw score is above average, so his grade equivalent score would be something like 6.3. This means his performance corresponds to what a sixth grader in the third month of school would, on the average, achieve.

Stanine Scores. Stanine scores are norm-referenced. "Stanine" is short for "standard nine." Raw scores are converted to a nine point scale. The number 5 is average, 9 is the top, and 1 is the bottom. Our fourth grader would have a stanine score of 8.

Informal Reading Inventories

Once again, we will go over specific approaches to assessment for each of the RICA Content Areas in the appropriate chapters. Now, though, we must review some information about Informal Reading Inventories (IRIs). An IRI generates information about several aspects of reading development.

An IRI is a battery, or collection, of tests administered individually to students. For an IRI, one adult gives the tests to one student. No two IRIs have to contain the same collection of tests. The selection of tests for the IRI depends on the student's reading level. For example, an IRI for a sixth grader with average ability would *not* include tests of concepts about print, phonemic awareness, and phonics. An IRI for a first grader with average ability would. Here are the types of tests generally included in an IRI:

Word Recognition Lists (described in this chapter)

Graded Reading Passages (described in this chapter)

Reading Interest Survey (described in Chapter 10)

Tests Measuring Concepts About Print (described in Chapter 4)

Phonemic Awareness Test (described in Chapter 3)

Phonics Tests (described in Chapter 5)

Structural Analysis Tests (described in Chapter 12)

Content Reading CLOZE Test (described in Chapter 7)

Vocabulary Tests (described in Chapter 12)

Spelling Tests (described in Chapter 6)

Word Recognition Lists

In this chapter, we will take a closer look at the word recognition lists and graded reading passages. The word recognition lists are sometimes called "graded word lists." These are lists of words, usually ten in each list. There is a list for every reading level. The first list, for kindergarteners is called the "preprimer" level, or "PP." It will have words like *the, am,* and *or.* The next list for kindergarteners, with slightly more difficult words, is at the "primer" level, "P." Then there is a list of words for every grade level from first grade to eighth grade. Some IRIs include word recognition lists for the high school grades, too. The words on the eighth grade list will be difficult, like *psychology* and *endorsement.* The word recognition lists from one IRI, the Bader Reading and Language Inventory (3rd edition) are in Appendix A at the end of this book.

Children are asked to read aloud each word. The word recognition lists serve three purposes: (1) they are used to provide a rough guess of the child's reading level so that whoever is administering the tests knows where to start on the graded reading passages; (2) the word recognition lists provide information on the child's "sight" vocabulary, the level of words the child can correctly identify; and (3) the child's performance will give you information about his or her ability to use sound-symbol relationships (phonics) to decode words. The child's errors will provide a partial picture of what letters and letter combinations the child knows and which ones he or she needs to learn.

A example of a teacher's scoring sheet for a third grader's performance on the Bader Graded Word Lists is included as Appendix B. Different IRIs will have different instructions for how to administer the word recognition lists. Basically, students read the words and the teacher records the results, placing a check by words read correctly, noting which words are read with hesitation, and writing the word a child says when he or she misidentifies a word.

Graded Reading Passages

The most important part of the IRI is the graded reading passages. Like the word recognition lists, the graded reading passages are provided for every reading level from preprimer for kindergarteners to eighth grade. Some IRIs include graded reading passages for the high school grades. Since the graded reading passages can be used in a number of ways, an IRI usually includes two or more passages for each grade. An example of one of the first grade passages from the Bader Reading and Language Inventory is included as Appendix C. A sixth grade passage is Appendix D.

The word recognition lists determine which passage is first administered to the student. The student then reads the passage aloud, and the teacher keeps a detailed record of the student's performance. Though many teachers can record what the student says while the student is reading, it is easier to tape record the child. This process will be used to do a miscue analysis. By looking at the student's errors we can gain a better understanding of how he or she reads. Patterns of errors will emerge and reveal how the child goes about decoding print. Errors fall into three categories.

Semantic errors. These are meaning-related errors, like reading *dad* for *father*. The student has relied too much on the semantic cueing system – and hasn't used graphophonemic clues. A child who repeatedly makes semantic errors understands what he or she is reading, but needs to be taught to use phonics skills to be sure that every word read makes sense from a graphophonemic sense (phonics is covered in Chapter 5).

Graphophonemic errors. *Graphophonemic* comes from the Greek words for *symbol* and *sound*. These are errors related to the sound-symbol relationships for English, like reading *feather* for *father*. The words sound alike, but *feather* wouldn't make sense in a sentence where the correct word is *father*. A child who repeatedly makes graphophonemic errors is either (a) reading word by word and depending too much on phonics to read each word or (b) reading a passage that is too difficult for him or her, doesn't understand what he or she is reading, and thus can only try to decode each word. Children who are reading word by word need to be taught to speed up (see Chapter 7). Children who don't use the meaning of the sentences and paragraphs to decode words need to be taught to use what are called contextual clues (see Chapter 12).

Syntactic Errors. To a linguist, syntax is the way words are placed in order in sentences. A syntactic error would be reading *into* for *through*. Both are prepositions. Syntactic errors make sense in that the error is the same part of speech as the correct word. As with semantic errors, a child who repeatedly makes syntactic errors needs to pay more attention to phonics, the sounds English letters make.

The most popular form of this miscue analysis is called a Running Record, which was developed in New Zealand. Each IRI, however, uses a different system for teachers to use to record the child's oral reading performance on the graded reading passages. One system is included as Appendix E. Scoring sheets for one child's oral reading are Appendix F.

After the child has read the passage aloud, he or she is then asked to answer some comprehension questions for the passage. The questions are included in the IRI examiner's manual. The teacher reads the questions and the child responds orally. An alternative for younger children in kindergarten, first grade, and second grade is for the teacher to ask the child to <u>retell</u> the story. The IRI provides a list of characters, places, and events in the passage the child should mention. This form of measuring comprehension, called a retelling, has been shown to work well.

Frustration, Instructional, and Independent Reading Levels

The administration of the graded reading passages of an IRI will allow the teacher determine each child's frustration, instructional, and independent reading levels. <u>This information is essential for teachers to know</u>. Different IRIs use different formulas, but those listed below are fairly standard.

Independent reading level. Books and stories at this level can be read and understood by the child without assistance by the teacher. A student's independent reading level is the <u>highest</u> passage for which the student reads aloud 98% or more of words correctly <u>and</u> answers 90% or more of the comprehension questions correctly.

Instructional reading level. Material at this level can be read and understood by the student with help from the teacher. The student's reading textbook (basal reader) should be at this level. The social studies and science textbooks should be at this reading level. A student's instructional reading level is the highest passage for which the students read aloud 90% or more of the words correctly <u>and</u> answer at least 60% of the comprehension questions correctly.

Frustration reading level. Books at this level <u>cannot</u> be read and understood by the child, even with help. (The child can <u>listen</u> to the teacher or someone else read material at this level and understand it.) For a passage at this level, the child correctly read aloud less than 90% of the words *or* did not answer 60% of the comprehension questions correctly.

Don't forget: To determine instructional and independent reading levels, you must know both (1) the percentage of words the child read aloud correctly and (2) the percentage of comprehension questions the child correctly answered.

The graded reading passages can also be used to determine the student's ability to comprehend what he or she has read silently. Then, the teacher has the student read the passage silently. The teacher asks the comprehension questions after the child finishes reading.

Chapter 2
Content Area 2:
Planning, Organizing, and Managing Reading Instruction

Introduction

S-ABCD

This Content Area describes the principles that should guide instruction at the *program* level. In other words, if someone were to observe a classroom over the entire school year, what consistent features would be present? The Content Specifications define five principles that teachers should follow when they plan, organize, and manage reading instruction:

(1) Instruction is driven by local and state content and performance **standards**

(2) Instruction is based on the results of ongoing **assessment**

(3) Instruction is **balanced**

(4) Instruction is **comprehensive** in scope

(5) Instruction is **differentiated** to fit the needs of all students

To memorize these principles, you might want to memorize the mnemonic **S-ABCD**.

Standards Driven

Teachers should plan instruction with the following goal: Every student in the classroom will meet the content and performance standards established by the local school district and the state of California. This is an important point because too many beginning teachers either have no sense of the ultimate goal of reading instruction or, even worse, think that the goal is simply to move through a basal reader and accompanying workbook page by page.

The California Department of Education and the State Board of Education have established English-Language Arts Content Standards for California Public Schools, Kindergarten through Grade Twelve. These content standards are statements of what every child is supposed to know and be able to do at each grade level. For example, first graders are supposed to be able to "distinguish long- and short-vowel sounds in orally stated single-syllable words (e.g., *bit/bite*)."

The California State Board of Education has yet to adopt performance standards in English-Language Arts. Performance standards will define the grade level at which each standard must be achieved. For example, for the standard mentioned in the previous paragraph, the performance standard could be the ability to distinguish 8 of 10 words similar to *bit/bite*.

The English-Language Arts Content Standards are important. Eventually, all textbooks purchased with money from the state of California will have to be aligned with these standards. Also, at some time in the future, California's assessment of K-12 students, the Standardized Testing and Reporting (STAR) program, will be aligned to these standards.

Many school districts, before the state standards were approved, developed their own standards in reading and the other language arts.

The bottom line is simple: Your job as a teacher is to raise your teaching standards to meet the state and district standards. All of your instructional decisions, the materials you choose, how you group students, should be aimed at enabling every student in your room to achieve each of the standards for your grade level.

The English-Language Arts Content Standards for California Public Schools: Kindergarten Through Grade Twelve can be purchased from the California Department of Education in Sacramento (800-995-4099). Or, you can read them online at the Schools of California Online Resources for Education (SCORE) web site at **http://score.rims.k12.ca.us**.

Ongoing Assessment

We covered this assessment principle in the previous chapter but it bears repeating. You will make instructional decisions on the basis of the results of ongoing assessment that utilizes a variety of assessment tools. For example, let us use the standard mentioned earlier. Suppose that your first graders can hear the difference in long and short vowel sounds in single syllable words (the difference between *bit/bite, bat/bait, bed/bead*). Ideally, you would test your students to determine who has achieved this standard and who has not. Those students who have met the standard will work on other reading activities while you provide direct instruction to what will likely be a small group study.

Balanced Instruction

Daily, the children in your classroom receive direct, explicit instruction in those reading skills and strategies they have not yet mastered and they have opportunities to *use* what they have learned. Direct, explicit lessons are best taught to small groups of students who share a common need. These are teacher-directed lessons, and though the teacher may use any of a number of resources, the objective of the lesson is to teach the reading skill or strategy. In this sense, the teaching is explicit in that the objective (the skill or strategy) is your focus. The opposite, and worthwhile approach, is for children to actually read something or write something that is a more authentic opportunity to acquire the skill or strategy. This is teaching the skill or strategy <u>indirectly, implicitly,</u> or in an <u>embedded</u> fashion.

The Content Specifications mention many types of activities which serve to balance direct, explicit teaching: listening to a story read aloud, playing a game with words, reading fiction and nonfiction independently, and writing stories and journal entries.

To elaborate more on distinguishing direct and indirect approaches to teaching, let us again use the example of the skill of distinguishing short and long vowels in single-syllable words when they are spoken. This is a phonemic awareness skill which has become one of the California English-Language Arts Content Standards. In a direct, explicit lesson, a small group of children, ideally no more than six, who have <u>not</u> acquired this skill would meet with the teacher. The teacher begins the lesson by reviewing the long and short vowel sounds ("the *a* makes two sounds, it says its own name in *main*, and makes another sound in *man*"). The teacher then says a pair of words, some with the same vowel sound (*gain/pain*) and some with different vowel sounds (*bet/beat*). The children are told to make some sort of signal, like tapping their heads, when they hear words that have different middle sounds.

To provide balance, this group of children and their classmates later in the day will listen as their teacher reads aloud Dr. Seuss' <u>The Cat in the Hat</u>. Later, the teacher will play a game with words that have the same vowel sound and rhyme, like *cat/hat*. The teacher's goal will be to enjoy good literature and have fun with language. Some children will, indirectly, improve their ability to identify and distinguish vowel sounds.

Comprehensive in Scope

Teachers should not get bogged down on any one component of a comprehensive reading program. Unfortunately, this happens. For example, neither a first grade teacher who does nothing but teach phonics nor a fifth grade teacher who lets her or his students read library books independently but does little else will provide adequate reading instruction for their respective students.

According to the Content Specifications, a comprehensive reading program will include (each RICA Content Area is in boldface):

(1) <u>Assessment</u>, using multiple measures, and conducted on an ongoing basis.

(2) The development of phonological awareness and other linguistic processes related to reading. This includes the development of <u>phonemic awareness</u>; <u>concepts about print</u>; <u>systematic, explicit phonics and other word identification strategies</u>, and <u>spelling</u>.

(3) The development of reading comprehension and independent reading. This includes <u>reading comprehension</u>; <u>literary response and analysis</u>; <u>content-area literacy</u>; and <u>independent reading</u>.

(4) Supporting reading through oral and written language development. This includes <u>an understanding of the relationships among reading, writing, and oral language</u>; the <u>development of vocabulary</u>; and <u>an understanding of the structure of the English language.</u>

Differentiated Instruction for Individuals and Groups

Because each child's needs are unique, teachers must differentiate instruction to meet individual differences. Assessment will inform the teacher of each child's strengths and weaknesses. Instruction becomes differentiated when a teacher no longer relies solely on "whole group" lessons. Thus, teachers will form <u>flexible</u> groups so children who share the need for a reading skill or strategy will be taught efficiently. Groups are flexible and because they exist for a single purpose will then be disbanded as soon as the teacher has completed the lessons planned for the group. Those students who are having particular difficulty will need <u>individualized instruction,</u> one-on-one sessions with the teacher. It is important that these one-on-one sessions be timely and are initiated as soon as the teacher sees that a child is falling behind his or her classmates.

To summarize, when it comes to grouping, some lessons will be taught to the whole group (teacher reading aloud and a skills lesson if all, or almost all, of the children in the room need it). Most direct, explicit instruction will be done in a small group format with children who share a common need. Finally, some instruction will be individualized.

The RICA Content Specifications state that differentiated instruction is essential because teachers should do what is necessary to ensure that all students achieve grade-level standards. The goal is to develop reading competence among all our students, including English language learners and students with special needs.

Chapter 3
Content Area 3:
Phonemic Awareness

Introduction

The Difference Between <u>Phonemic Awareness</u> and <u>Phonics</u>

<u>Phonemic awareness</u> is the "conscious awareness that words are made up of individual speech sounds" (from the RICA Content Specifications). When a child can identify *duck* and *luck* as rhyming words or say that *duck* has three sounds and they are /d/, /u/, /k/, he or she is phonemically aware. Phonemic awareness is an awareness of the sounds of the language. Phonemic awareness can be taught without print. The development of phonemic awareness is an important goal for kindergarten teachers.

<u>Phonics</u> is knowledge of letter/sound correspondences, knowing, for example, that in the word *phonics* the letters *ph* make the /f/ sound.

Know the Phonemic Awareness Tasks

A student is phonemically aware if he or she is able to perform <u>all</u> of the following tasks:

Sound matching. This is an ability to identify or provide words that have the same sound in the beginning, middle, or final position as a target word. For example, a teacher says, "The word is *dog*. *Dog*. What is another word that starts the same way as *dog*?" A correct response in this sound matching task would be *dad* or *don't*.

Sound isolation. In this phonemic awareness task, the student must identify which sound occurs in the beginning, middle or end of a word. For example, a teacher would ask, "Which sound starts these words, *tea, top, take*?" The correct answer would be, of course, /t/. (Linguists, the people who study language, identify a single sound by putting a simple letter between slash marks, / /. This is because a single sound may have more than one spelling. For example, the *c* in *cat* and the *ck* in *duck* both make the sound /k/.)

Sound blending. The student must be able to manipulate individual sounds by combining them to form a word. The teacher says, "What word is made of these three sounds, /k/ (pause), /a/ (pause), /t/?" The student should respond, *cat*.

Sound addition and substitution. In a sound addition and substitution task students should be able to substitute a sound every time a target sound appears in a phrase. For example, the teacher says, "Fe-fi-fiddly-i-o. Substitute *z*." The child would respond, "Ze-zi-ziddly-i-o."

Sound segmentation. Sound segmentation is the most difficult phonemic awareness task. The teacher says a word and the child must identify each separate sound in the word. For example, the teacher says, "*Pop.* Tell me the sounds in *pop*." The correct answer would be /p/, /o/, /p/.

Research on Phonemic Awareness

Longitudinal studies of reading acquisition have demonstrated that the acquisition of phonemic awareness is highly predictive of success in learning to read, in particular, in predicting success in learning to decode. In fact, phonemic awareness abilities developed before or in kindergarten appear to be the best single predictor of successful reading acquisition.

Why? Phonemic awareness is the foundation for understanding the alphabetic principle that English letters represent sounds.

Definitions

For both this Content Area and the Content Area 5 (Systematic, Explicit Phonics and Other Word Identification Strategies) you will need to know the following definitions.

The alphabetic principle is that distinctive speech sounds of a language, called phonemes, are represented by symbols called letters.

Phoneme. Most linguists would define a phoneme as a speech sound in a language that signals a difference in meaning. /v/ is an English phoneme because there is a difference between *vote* and *boat*. A simpler definition is: Phonemes are the smallest units of speech and they are written as graphemes (letters). They are indicated with / /. Remember: Sometimes a single phoneme /k/ is represented by two letters (*ck* in *duck*).

Vowels are sounds made when the air leaving your lungs is vibrated in the voice box and there is a clear passage from the voice box to your mouth. In English, the following letters are always vowels: *a, e, i, o, u.* Two letters are sometimes vowels: *y,* in words like *sky,* and *w* in words like *cow.* Vowel sounds are said to be long when they "say their own name" as in *bake* and *bite.* Short vowels occur in words like *cat, pet, bit, cot, but.* R-controlled vowels are neither long nor short, as in the sounds *a* makes in *car, e* as in *her, i* as in *fir, u* as in *fur,* and *o* as in *for.*

Consonants are speech sounds that occur when the airflow is obstructed in some way in your mouth.

Onsets and rimes. In a syllable the onset is the initial consonant and the rime is the vowel and any consonants that follow.

Word	Onset	Rime
Cats	/k/	/atz/
In	-	in
Spring	spr	ing

Remember: Onsets and rimes occur in <u>syllables</u>. Every syllable has a rime. Some syllables also have an onset.

Phonograms are rimes that have the same spelling. Words that share the same phonogram are <u>word families</u>. Rime or phonogram: *at*. Word family: *cat, bat, sat*

Blends are the combined sounds of two or three sounds. Examples of consonant blends are: *pl* in play and *spr* in *spring*. Remember: The *bl* in *blend* is a blend!

Digraphs are combination of sounds that make a unique sound, unlike the sound made by any of the individual letters within the digraph. For example, *ph* in *phone* and *sh* in *share*. Don't forget: The *ph* in *digraph* is a digraph!

Diphthongs are glided sounds made by such vowel combinations as *oi* in *oil* and *oy* in *boy*. When pronouncing a diphthong, the tongue starts in one position and rapidly moves to another.

Beginning, Medial, Final refer to locations of phonemes. *Medial* means *middle*. *Cat*: beginning /k/, medial /a/, ending /t/.

How to Assess Phonemic Awareness

In tests of phonemic awareness, the teacher talks, the student listens, and then the student says something. No print is involved. Older tests referred to these tests as <u>auditory discrimination</u>.

One widely-used test is the <u>Yopp-Singer Test of Phoneme Segmentation</u>. In this test, the teacher says 22 words (*dog, keep, fine, no*). The child must provide each sound of the word in order. So, when the teacher says *dog*, the correct response is /d/, /o/, /g/. Remember, sound segmentation is the most difficult phonemic awareness task. So, if a student does well on the Yopp-Singer Test of Phoneme Segmentation, you probably can assume he or she can do the other phonemic awareness tasks as well.

To do a complete job of assessing phoneme awareness, teachers should test each of the tasks: sound matching, sound isolation, sound blending, sound addition and substitution, and sound segmentation. It is easy for teachers to develop simple tests of these tasks. For example, to develop a test of sound isolation, the teacher would actually make three sub tests, one for identifying sounds in the beginning position, another for identifying medial sounds, and one for ending sounds. For a test of medial sounds the teacher would need to create a list of 15–20 words with different medial sounds (which would be different vowel sounds, such as *bet, feet, cat, take*, etc.). For each word, the teacher would say, "Listen to me say this word, *feet. Feet. Feet*. What is the middle sound in *feet*?"

How to Teach Phonemic Awareness

The Content Specifications mention <u>implicit</u> and <u>explicit</u>. Implicit, or indirect, teaching refers to the use of books with rhymes and wordplay, chants, songs, and games. Phonemic awareness can be developed as a result of participating in lessons that focus on the sounds of words. Explicit, or direct, teaching refers to lessons with the stated objective of developing phonemic awareness. When children are first challenged with one of the phonemic awareness tasks, it is important that the teacher first <u>model</u> the performance he or she wishes the students to demonstrate.

Implicit (Indirect) Teaching of Phonemic Awareness

Books with wordplay. These are books with texts that rhyme and/or feature alliteration (consonants) and assonance (a partial rhyme in which the stressed vowel sounds are alike but the consonant sounds are unalike: *late* and *make*). Examples: <u>Each Peach Pear Plum</u> by Ahlberg and Ahlberg and <u>Faint Frogs Feeling Feverish and Other Terrifically Tantalizing Tongue Twisters</u> by Obligado.

The teacher reads the book aloud and then asks questions or makes comments that focus on the phonemes in the text: "Did you notice how *cat* and *hat* rhyme?" Or, "This book is fun because of all the words that begin with the /m/ sound. Let's say them."

Rhyming games. Children love to say words that rhyme. The goal is to have children chant rhyming words and then generate new rhyming words. Children should learn and sing nursery rhymes and songs that are full of rhymes.

Explicit (Direct) Teaching of Phonemic Awareness

Many children will come to school with phonemic awareness. Others will acquire it with, seemingly, very little effort. For other children, however, acquiring phonemic awareness is a significant challenge. Kindergarten and first grade teachers should assess their students to find out who is having difficulty with phonemic awareness tasks. For example, a kindergarten teacher has identified six children who have difficulty with sound isolation. They don't seem to hear middle sounds. The teacher should teach direct, explicit lessons on sound isolation to this group of six students. For these lessons, the teacher's objective is the development of the ability to isolate and identify middle sounds.

Sound matching. To teach sound matching, there are a number of possible lessons a teacher could plan. For example, a teacher could have a box with toys and stuffed animals. The teacher provides the target sound, /s/, and says, "Find something in the box that starts with the /s/ sound." The children would look for the plastic snake.

Sound isolation. This is really the reverse from sound matching. In sound isolation, the children are given a word and asked to tell which sound occurs at the beginning, middle, or end of the word. The teacher could have a list of words that all have long vowels in the medial position: *cake, day, late, leap, feel, vote, coal, bite, like.* To model the desired response, at the beginning of the lesson the teacher would say each word and then say the medial sound ("*leap, leap*, the middle sound is /e/). At some point, the teacher just says the word and the children have to provide the medial sound.

Or the teacher could simply ask the question, "What's the sound that starts these words: *tennis, tackle, terrific*?"

Sound blending. In the simplest lessons to teach sound blending, the teacher says the sounds with only brief pauses in between each sound. The children then guess the word ("Which word am I thinking of? Its sounds are /b/, /a/, and /t/." The answer would be *bat* or *tab*.). Sound blending is more difficult if the teacher pauses for long periods, like five or six seconds, between each sound. The most difficult sound blending lessons challenge students to take "scrambled" sounds and rearrange them into words. For example, the teacher would say, "What word is made of these sounds, /a/, /t/, /b/?" Again, the answer would be *bat* or *tab*.

Another good way to teach sound blending is to ask children to blend an onset and a rime. For example, use the rime of *–ank*. The teacher would say /b/ and *–ank*. The children should say, *bank*. Then, blend *th* with *–ank*, and get *thank*, *cr* with *–ank* and get *crank*.

Sound addition and substitution. Though this task is referred to as "addition and substitution," it seems to me to be a matter of simply asking children to substitute one sound for another. The hardest part of this for the teacher is finding phrases that work for this type of task. The easiest ones would be one-word substitutions. The teacher says, "*Cat, cat, cat.* Let's substitute the /b/ sound for the /k/ sound. We get *bat, bat, bat*." Then, the teacher might try simple alliterations (all start with the same consonant sounds). For example, the teacher says, *be, bo, ba, bu, bi* (in this example of nonsense words, all the vowels are long). The students would then chant, *be, bo, ba, bu, bi.* The teacher then says, lets substitute /k/ for the /b/. The students would then chant *ke, ko, ka, ku, ki.* Obviously, it becomes more fun to do sound addition and substitution if you use a well-known chant from a song, like fe-fi-fiddly-i-o from "I've Been Working on the Railroad."

Segmentation. This is the most difficult of the phonemic awareness tasks. Children are challenged to isolate and identify the sounds in a spoken word. To teach this directly, the teacher should start with words with only two sounds. Remember, the teacher should always model the desired student behavior first. The teacher would say, "I am going to say a word and then slowly say the sounds in the word. *Bee.* (pause) /b/ (pause) /e/. Then the teacher would ask the students to say the sounds in two-sound words. After the children have shown they can segment two-sound words, then lessons should focus on words with three sounds. The lesson challenges children to segment words with minimal differences, like *cap*, *cat*, and *cab*.

Chapter 4
Content Area 4:
Concepts About Print

Introduction

What Are Concepts About Print?

"Concepts about print refer to an understanding of how letters, words, and sentences are represented in written language" (RICA Content Specifications). To learn how to read, children must acquire these concepts. They should be learned by the time the child leaves kindergarten. The actual phrase "concepts about print" was coined by the New Zealand educator Marie Clay, who developed a test of concepts about print. The concepts are:

Print carries meaning. This is the most important concept. Children have acquired this concept when they know that words are used to transmit messages – stories in picture books, product names in advertisements, and labels on things like bathroom doors. It is possible to know this concept and <u>not</u> be able to read the printed words in the text. For example, many children who have been read to before they come to school will take a favorite picture book, sit down with it, and tell the story as they look at the pictures. These children cannot read every word on the page – but they have acquired the concept that the printed words <u>are</u> the story.

Directionality of English and tracking of print. Students have acquired the concept of directionality when they understand that words/symbols written in English are read left to right and top to bottom. Tracking is evidence that this concept has been learned, as the child is able to point to the next word that should be read.

Sentence, word, and letter representation. Again, this concept is <u>not</u> the ability to read words and sentences or identify letters. Rather, it is the knowledge of the <u>differences</u> between letters, words, and sentences. To fully acquire this concept children must know how many letters are in a word. A child who has acquired this concept knows <u>word boundaries</u>, that is, how many words there are in a line of text. Finally, children need to know where sentences end and begin, which requires recognition of end punctuation (., !, ?).

Book orientation. This is knowledge of where the cover of a book is, the difference between the author's name and the title, and where the story starts.

The RICA Content Specifications include **letter recognition** as a sub topic under concepts about print. It will be dealt with in a separate section at the end of this chapter.

Children Who Do Not Understand "Concepts About Print" Must Be Taught Them

Many children will acquire all the concepts about print without direct instruction, especially if their parents or someone else has spent a great deal of time reading to them at home. Other children will acquire concepts about print by taking part in classroom activities like listening to their teacher read aloud, through shared book experiences, and by dictating stories which are transcribed by an adult.

The RICA Content Specifications, however, state "Teachers need to know that if a student does not demonstrate understanding of concepts about print and the written language system, then these concepts must be explicitly taught." Teachers should assess their students. Those who need help acquiring concepts about print should be taught them in a direct, explicit manner.

How to Assess Concepts About Print

Concepts About Print Test

Marie Clay from New Zealand developed the *Concepts About Print* test. The *Concepts About Print* test is very popular and is used in many California kindergarten classrooms. To administer the test, the teacher uses one of two special books, <u>Sand</u> or <u>Stones</u>. The books have some pages with the print upside down, some words with the letters reversed, and some lines of print in odd configurations. The teacher asks the student to do things like point to the front of the book, to identify where the teacher should start to read on a page, and to recognize the beginning and ending of a word. The test measures book orientation, directionality, beginning and ending of a story, word sequence, and recognition of punctuation and capital letters.

If you have a question on RICA that requires you to write about assessing concepts about print, be sure to mention Clay's *Concepts About Print* test.

Informal Assessment by the Teacher

It is relatively easy for classroom teachers to assess concepts about print by using any picture book that has at least three or four lines of text displayed in conventional form on most pages. The teacher asks students to perform tasks and keeps a record of the results.

For example, to assess directionality and tracking of print, the teacher, at the start of a new page, would ask the child to point to where the teacher should start reading. The child should point to the first word on the first line of the text. Then, as the teacher reads slowly, the child would be asked to put his or her finger under each succeeding word, to track the flow of the print. To assess word boundaries, the teacher could cover up all but one line of text and ask the child how many words are on that line.

How to Teach Concepts About Print

Implicit (Indirect) Teaching of Concepts About Print

Reading aloud to students. Reading aloud will teach many children the concept that print carries meaning. Reading aloud also will help children recognize the covers of books. If the teacher is reading aloud a standard-sized picture book to a class of 20 students, then the children will not be able to see each word of the text. This means reading aloud will not teach directionality or sentence, word, and letter representation. Teachers should read aloud to the students every day, select high quality books, and read with enthusiasm and panache.

The shared book experience. With shared book experiences, teachers attempt to achieve with a group of children what has long been accomplished when an adult shares a picture book with one child. When an adult, typically a parent, sits and reads a book to and with a child, this is called lap reading, though unless the child is a relative, you do not actually let him or her sit in your lap. The shared book experience was named by New Zealand educator Don Holdaway. The goals of a shared book experience are to discover good books, to see that reading books is fun, and to teach concepts about print. The shared book experience is a particularly powerful activity because it has the potential to teach all of the concepts about print.

Teachers use big books for shared book experiences. Big books are just that, oversized picture books measuring at least 15 x 23 inches. Many big books have been written with predictable phrases or words as a part of the text. Predictable books are ideal for shared book experiences. Familiar predictable books whose predictable plot or language pattern is popular include books such as The House That Jack Built by Jenny Stow, The Judge by Harve Zemach, and The Napping House by Audrey Wood. A shared book experience usually has the following components:

(1) Introduction (prereading) – Look at cover, point out features of the book (like author name, illustrator name, title page, later (publisher). Then ask, "What do you think this book will be about?" or some other predictive questions.

(2) The teacher then reads the story with full dramatic punch, maybe overdoing it a little. The children join in on the predictable text. The teacher may pause to encourage predictions or comments. If the teacher wants to stress directionality and tracking of print, he or she will point to every word as he or she reads it.

(3) A discussion occurs before, during, or after the text reading. Children ask questions, or talk about favorite parts or characters.

(4) The story is then reread on subsequent days with the whole group, in smaller groups, with student pairs or to individual students – acting out and enjoying the language patterns.

Language Experience Approach (LEA). The LEA is intended to develop and support children's reading and writing abilities. Children share an experience such as a field trip to the zoo and then dictate an account of that experience to an adult, who records it verbatim. An LEA should record a personal experience that is vicarious and will provide the child with a great deal to dictate. Together, the adult and child read the dictated text. The text is saved and bound in a child's personal reading book. Class experiences can be dictated by several children whose comments are collected on chart paper. The class then reads the dictated "story" together and the LEA is displayed in the classroom.

The LEA will teach most of the concepts about print. Repeated experiences will help children acquire the big idea – that print carries meaning. Teachers can have children follow along with their fingers as they read aloud. This will teach directionality and tracking of print. The LEA also is a good way to teach sentence, word, and letter representation. Portions of the dictated narrative can be reread, with emphasis on identifying sentences, words, and letters. The LEA, however, cannot be used to teach book orientation. LEA experiences also can be used to teach many other things like letter recognition, phonics, and vocabulary. After the teacher reads the dictated text, and the teacher and child read it together, any portion of the text can be used for a directed lesson.

Environmental print. "Environmental print" refers to printed messages that people encounter in ordinary, daily living. This includes: milk cartons, bumper stickers, candy wrappers, toy boxes, cereal boxes, billboards, menus, and T shirts. Teachers should display examples of environmental print on bulletin boards and learning centers. Once displayed, children will see that print carries meaning. Lessons can be based on the letters, words, phrases, and sentences that appear on the items. Obviously, environmental print can't be used to teach book orientation and it may not work for directionality because many product labels, advertisements, and T-shirts display words in atypical formats, with letters running over the surface in strange configurations.

Print-rich environment. All classrooms should be "print-rich," with plenty of examples of written language on display. For kindergarteners and first graders, this print-rich environment will help them acquire concepts about print. Children can then "read the room." There are many ways to create this environment:

* Labels/Captions. Classroom items should be labeled, like desks, chairs, the clock, and the windows. Bulletin board displays should have easy-to-read captions.

* Morning Message. The morning message is written on chart paper, in large letters, and provides an overview of the day's activities. For example, "Today is Wednesday, October 11. At ten o'clock we will see a movie about farm animals. We will use the finger paints to make pictures with the colors blue, yellow, and red." The teacher reads the morning message to the students and talks about the day and upcoming events. Students share news with the class. Sometimes, the teacher may wait to write the message

until the children are seated in front of an easel with blank chart paper. Then the morning message provides an opportunity for children to see how words become print.

The morning message can be used to teach directionality; letter, word, and sentence representation; and the concept that print carries meaning. The morning message, of course, cannot be used to teach book orientation.

* Mailboxes. Classroom mailboxes or "cubbies" can be made of milk cartons. They can be used to hold messages as students write to their classmates and the teacher writes to students (for many kindergarteners and first graders, the messages may have to be dictated and transcribed by an adult). Children discover the social purposes of language and that print carries meaning.

Explicit (Direct) Teaching of Concepts About Print

The previous activities will be enough for many children to acquire all the concepts about print they need. For others, you will need to plan direct lessons. For lessons on book orientation, you can use any picture book, assuming the children can see all the words. Big books are ideal for teaching book orientation to a larger group of children. For the other concepts about print, you can use any of the texts mentioned previously: picture books, environmental print, the child's dictated LEA narratives, or the morning message. The key is that in a direct, explicit lesson, you have as an objective one of the concepts about print. The concept won't be something children "just pick up" but do need to be taught specifically.

For example, for a child having difficulty with the directionality and tracking of English print, the teacher would select a picture book. First, the book would be read and enjoyed. Then, the teacher would return to the first page of the text and reread it with the child, guiding the child's finger underneath each word as it is read. For a lesson on word representation, the teacher could work with the morning message. In a direct lesson, children would listen to the teacher read a line, and then chant and clap the number of words on the line.

Teaching the Names of the Letters

Teachers should use a variety of methods to teach children the names of the letters. Please note that we are discussing teaching the names of the letters, not the sounds letters make (covered in the next chapter).

Use the names of the children and favorite things (like toys). The teacher could display a large letter on the blackboard, like a *J*, and then ask everybody with names beginning with *J* to stand underneath the *J*. Teachers can ask children to arrange toys or common classroom objects by letters they begin with. Under *B*, for example, we would have books, balls, and Beanie Babies™.

Singing the alphabet. Many generations of children have sung the alphabet song. The important thing to remember is that to teach the names of the letters, the song needs to be sung slowly as someone points to each letter.

ABC books. Teachers should read aloud books that are organized by the letters of the alphabet. There are dozens of these ABC books. Two of my favorites are <u>26 Letters and 99 Cents</u> by Tana Hoban and <u>Animalia</u> by Graeme Base.

Practice writing both upper and lower case letters. Children will learn the names of the letters as they practice writing them. These direct, explicit lessons should include clear instruction on how to make the letters and a reasonable amount of time for practice. Remember, kindergarteners are only five years old and thus most have not developed the fine motor skills that allow them to write letters perfectly.

Tactile and kinesthetic methods. For those children who have difficulty associating the names to the letters or have difficulty writing them, tactile and kinesthetic lessons are in order. "Tactile" refers to touch. Tactile lessons include the use of concrete materials to practice the configurations of letters. For example, children could make three-dimensional letters out of modeling clay or trace their fingers over letters cut out of sand paper. "Kinesthetic" refers to motion. Kinesthetic lessons ask children to make exaggerated movements with their hands and arms, as they pretend to write letters that are two feet in height in the air.

Chapter 5
Content Area 5:
Systematic, Explicit Phonics and Other Word Identification Strategies

Introduction

Definitions

Word identification strategies are the "tools" readers use to recognize words. Word identification is the ability to say, or decode a word correctly. Please note that word identification does not mean knowing what the word means. Helping children expand their knowledge of word meanings is covered in Chapter 12 (Vocabulary). The RICA Content Specifications mention the following word identification strategies that children can use:

Phonics. A knowledge of phonics means having the ability to make the correct association between the sounds and the symbols of a language. Using the Greek roots for symbol and sound, these are often called graphophonic relationships.

Morphology. To a linguist, morphology is the study of word formation. Children use morphological clues to identify words when they rely on root words, prefixes, and suffixes. Using these morphological clues is also called structural analysis. All lessons on morphology should involve teaching the meaning of root words, prefixes, and suffixes, so we will discuss the use of morphological clues to both identify and understand the meanings of words in Chapter 12 (Vocabulary).

Context clues. In many instances, children can figure out a word they don't know if they know the meanings of the words surrounding the unknown word. When children do this, they have used the context of the sentence or paragraph to identify the words. The use of context clues, which will allow children to both identify and know the meaning of an unknown word, will be covered in Chapter 12 (Vocabulary).

Sight words. Children should be taught to identify some words as whole units, without breaking the word down by phonics or morphology. Two types of words should be taught as sight words: words that have irregular spelling patterns and words that appear frequently in printed English (which are called high-frequency words).

The Importance of Teaching Phonics Directly and Explicitly

To the people who designed RICA, the different word identification strategies are not of equal importance. The RICA Content Specifications make it clear that all primary grade teachers should teach children to identify words through phonics. Phonics instruction should have the following characteristics:

Instruction should be systematic and organized. This means that teachers should have a clear list of the sound-symbol relationships students at their grade level should know. Students should be assessed to determine which sound-symbol relationships they have mastered and which they need to learn. Sound-symbol relationships should be taught in a sequence which moves from simple to complex linguistic units: start with phonemes, move to onsets and rimes, then to letter combinations, and finally to syllables.

Instruction should be direct and explicit. The people who created RICA were concerned that too many teachers appeared to either teach phonics in a haphazard manner or not teach it at all. While it is true that some children will acquire some sound-symbol relationships with seemingly little effort as they take part in activities like shared book experiences and the language experience approach, most children will need to be taught phonics directly. In a direct, explicit lesson, the teacher's objective is to teach a sound-symbol relationship. These lessons are best taught to small groups of children who share the need to learn the same sound-symbol relationship.

Don't teach rules. The object of phonics instruction is not to teach children rules (i.e., when two vowels go walking, the first does the talking) or to teach six-year-old children the meanings of words like *digraph* and *diphthong*. Rather, the purpose of phonics instruction is to teach children the most regular and common sound-symbol relationships in the English language.

How to Assess Phonics

To completely assess students in phonics, teachers should administer tests that ask students to (1) encode and decode in (2) isolation and in context. There are many available phonics tests teachers can choose from. Most commercially published IRIs include phonics tests. Basal reading textbook series often come with a set of phonics tests teachers can use. Teachers can develop their own phonics tests, and this isn't particularly difficult for a decoding in isolation test. The teacher simply needs to come up with a list of words that share the same sound-symbol relationship. Let's look at each type of phonics test.

Decode in isolation. In this type of test, the child is presented a list of words and asked to read them. For example, if a teacher wanted to see which of her students knows the sound the *a* makes in the medial position in a one-syllable word, the test might consist of the following words: *mat, map, dad, pan, bad*. The teacher records what the child says for each word. If, for example, the child misidentified *mat* and substituted a long *e* sound, the teacher would write *meet* next to *mat*. Some IRIs include decoding in isolation tests with nonsense words (*fap, fep, fup*). This provides a "control" on the test because the child must use his or her phonics skills to figure the word out, he or she cannot get the word correct because he or she knows it as a sight word. A teacher, however, should never rely solely on tests of nonsense words, because our goal is to see if children can understand the sound-symbol relationships in the words he or she will read every day.

Decode in context. This is the most important phonics test because it asks students to read part of a story or an informational article. Students read a passage, several sentences in two or three paragraphs, aloud. The teacher keeps a record of the child's miscues, looking for words that are misidentified. The teacher especially looks for sound-symbol patterns that are missed repeatedly (for example, a child missed *felt* and *belt*, two words that share the *–elt* rime). This type of test, as you remember, is done as part of an Informal Reading Inventory.

Encode in isolation. The traditional spelling test is an encoding in isolation task. The teacher reads words aloud and the child writes them.

Encode in context. In this type of test the child writes a few sentences or a paragraph and the teacher analyzes the child's writing to see which sound-symbol relationships have not been learned.

How to Teach Phonics

Explicit (Direct) Teaching of Phonics

There are two general approaches to the explicit, direct teaching of phonics: whole-to-part (also called analytic phonics) and part-to-whole (also called synthetic phonics). Both approaches have supporters. Some basal reading textbook series feature part-to-whole lessons in their workbooks (Houghton Mifflin), while others rely heavily on part-to-whole lessons (Open Court). If you have a child who needs direct lessons in phonics, you should try one type of lesson and stay with it if it works. If the lessons aren't successful, try the other approach.

Whole-to-part lessons. Whole-to-part lessons start with sentences and then "work back" to the sound-symbol relationship that is the focus of the lesson. Here is what one lesson would look like with the goal of teaching the *sh* digraph at the end of words:

(1) Present a set of sentences on a piece of chart paper or on the blackboard, each sentence having a word with the common element. Underline the target word.

My mom went to the bank and came home with a lot of <u>cash</u>.
We went to the market and bought some <u>fish</u> and potatoes.
I helped her <u>mash</u> the potatoes.
After dinner, my brother Fred broke a <u>dish</u>.

(2) Students read each sentence aloud with the teacher. Then, the students read aloud the underlined word (*cash, fish, mash, dish*).

(3) Then the teacher says, "There is something about the underlined words that is the same, what is it?" The children should note they all end with *sh*. If they don't, tell them.

(4) The focus is now on the sound-symbol relationship. The teacher writes the letters *sh* on the board and, as the teacher points to the letters, the children make the appropriate sound.

(5) The children then reread the target words one more time.

Part-to-whole lessons. Part-to-whole lessons begin with the sound and then build words. The teaching sequence would be:

(1) The teacher writes the symbol on the board (*sh*) and tells children the sound that it makes.

(2) The children say the target sound each time the teacher points to it.

(3) Then the teacher shows letter combinations that can be added to the sound to make words. So the teacher would write *ca, fi, ma, di* on cards large enough for students to easily see them. The teacher places these cards in front of the *sh* written on the blackboard. The children would then blend the sounds to make a word (for example, *ca* and *sh* are read as *cash*).

Implicit (Indirect) Teaching of Phonics

The same activities that teachers use to teach phonemic awareness and concepts about print can be used to indirectly teach phonics. The important thing, of course, is to help children associate the relationships between letters and the sounds they make.

The shared book experience. With big books, children can see the words their teacher is reading aloud. Many shared book experiences end with an informal phonics lesson. The teacher might go back to a page that has rhyming words, point to the words, and have the children say them with him or her. Sometimes the words in a story can serve as the basis for a direct lesson. For example, after reading <u>The Cat In The Hat</u> by Dr. Seuss, the teacher may want to follow with a lesson on the *–at* rime.

Language play with rhymes and chants. Rhymes and chants can be used to teach sound-symbol relationships. If the goal is to teach phonics rather than phonemic awareness, then the children must see the words they are chanting (remember, phonemic awareness is simply <u>hearing</u> the sounds). For example, to teach the *br* consonant blend, the teacher could write the following tongue twister on a piece of chart paper: *Brilliant Brenda broke the brand new brush.* Read the twister aloud together (which is called <u>choral reading</u>). Then underline the *br*. Say the twister slowly and point to the *br* in each word.

Morning message, environmental print, children's names, things in the room. All of these print strategies can be used to teach phonics by simply calling attention to the sounds made by letters. For example, the children might be challenged to make a list of all the things in the room that start with the letter *p* (*pencils, people, paper*, etc.). The words are written on the board, and the target sound-symbol relationship highlighted (in this case, the *p* at the beginning of each word is underlined).

Sight Words

Phonics is not the only word identification strategy students should use. In the chapter on vocabulary (Chapter 12), we will discuss the use of contextual clues and the morphemic structure of words. In addition, however, every child should learn a large number of "sight words," words than can be recognized instantly without reliance on some other word identification strategy. There are four sources that expose children to sight words: (1) High-frequency words that appear most frequently in the printed texts children read (*as, the, of*). Many lists are available that identify these "high-frequency" words, like Edward Fry's List of 240 "Instant Words." (2) Words with "irregular" spellings, like *dove* and *great*. (3) Words that children want to know, usually because they want to use them in their writing (*dinosaur, Burger King*). (4) Words that are introduced in content-area lessons in social studies and science (*insect, butterfly*).

It is easy **to assess** children's knowledge of sight words. Teachers should give children tests on sight words both in <u>isolation</u> and in <u>context</u>. In isolation, sight words are displayed to a child, either on flash cards or on a list, and the child reads them. It is important to determine if the child can read the words in context as well. When children read aloud, from the graded passages in an IRI or from a story in a basal reader, and the teacher records the performance with a miscue analysis, the teacher can check to see which sight words were read correctly.

There are many ways to teach children sight words.

Word banks. A word bank is a child's personal collection of words that she knows well enough to recognize in isolation. The words are printed on small cards and kept in a small plastic bag or container (it is best if the teacher writes the words). Start with the child's name and other words the child is likely to know (names of a pet, brother, the street where he or she lives). The teacher and the child then add words from each of the sources listed above: high frequency words, words the child wants to know, and content-area words. When the word bank grows to about 100 words it becomes unwieldy and should be translated into a personal dictionary in book form (a page for each letter, words with the same beginning letter on a page).

Word walls. Primary grade teachers use a variety of word walls to display words that the children are using in the classroom. Some word walls are large pieces of chart paper with a topic written in the middle (i.e., *Insects*) and related words written around the topic. Other word walls are alphabet charts with space above each letter for several words. During the first week of school the teacher adds the children's names to this word wall (*Andy* and *Abigail* go above the *A*, *Benito* and *Brittney* above the *B*, etc.). Then, high-frequency and content-area words can be added.

Explicit (direct) teaching of sight words. A whole-to-part approach to teaching sight words would go as follows:

(1) First, the teacher would select three or four words to be learned (*who, want, there, your*).

(2) Then, the teacher would write each word in a sentence, preferably in somewhat of a story format, with the target words underlined:
> "*Who* has my ball?" Matt asked. "I *want* it back."
> "*There* it is," Janet said. "*Your* coat is on top of it."

(3) The teacher would read aloud the sentences, pointing to each word as it is read.

(4) The children then read the story aloud with the teacher. Have the children read the story aloud with you.

(5) The teacher then writes each target word on the board, points to one word at a time, pronounces it, asks the children to spell it, and then say it.

(6) As a follow-up, the words can be added to the children's word banks. The words can also be written on flashcards which can be used to review the words.

Chapter 6
Content Area 6:
Spelling Instruction

Introduction

The RICA Content Specifications state that spelling knowledge is closely related to word identification skills. Children who have mastered phonics skills – and know which letters are used to represent sounds – tend to be good spellers. Knowing how to spell also helps children expand their vocabularies and enhance their ability to write.

The RICA Content Specifications use the phrase orthographic patterns, which are the frequently occurring letter combinations of English spelling (i.e., the rime –ight, the suffix –tion).

As with all the RICA content areas, teachers are expected to know how to assess spelling development and use a variety of instructional strategies to teach children how to spell.

Finally, a word or two about "invented spelling." Many teachers have misunderstood this concept and my suggestion is that you not use this phrase when writing your answers to the RICA essay questions. It is clear from the RICA Content Specifications that the people who developed RICA were concerned about teachers who viewed incorrect spelling as "no big deal." Invented spelling, of course, was never a goal of teaching. It is something that happens when young children who have not learned all the orthographic patterns of English are encouraged to begin writing. Every teacher's goal should be to move every child toward conventional spelling by helping him or her master the patterns of English spelling. Specifically, instruction needs to fit the stages of spelling development that are described below.

How to Assess Spelling Development

Stages of Spelling Development

The RICA Content Specifications state that beginning teachers should be "able to analyze and interpret students' spelling to assess their stages of spelling development . . . and to use that information to plan appropriate spelling instruction." Four stages of spelling development are identified: pre-phonetic, phonetic, transitional, and conventional.

It is important to note that, as with any developmental stage theory, sometimes children don't fit neatly into these four categories. If a child is on the cusp of one of these stages, he or she might appear to be in two of the stages at the same time. Also, the jump from one stage to another doesn't occur overnight; children gradually move from one stage to another.

Knowing the child's level of development is important because it will tell you what type of instruction the child needs. Finally, your goal as a teacher is to move children through the stage they are in and on to the next stage. Your goal is not to immediately bring all children to the ultimate level of achievement – conventional spelling.

Pre-phonetic. Children at this level do not write at least one letter for each sound. Some sounds in words are not represented. The child's first attempts at writing will typically reveal no understanding of the alphabetic principle. Words will be represented by letter-like scribbles. Then, children begin to understand that words are represented by letters. So, the child will choose any convenient letter or combinations of letters to represent a word. *Cat* may be spelled *ABD*. Eventually, some of the sounds of the word are represented, but others are missing. *Banana* is spelled *baa*.

This stage is sometimes subdivided into the pre-communicative and semi-phonetic sub stages. Pre-communicative spelling shows no understanding that letters represent sounds. If letters appear, they are randomly assigned. Semi-phonetic spellers are aware of the alphabetic principle – they know that words are composed of letters. The child, however, does not have at least one letter to represent each sound. The child's writing is difficult, if not impossible, to read because many sounds in words are not represented.

Example: *MoICod spMNaido* [Child read this as "me next to a tree."]

Phonetic. Phonetic spellers know that letters represent sounds and at least one letter represents each sound in a word. The problem is, of course, that many times spellers do not choose the right letter or combination of letters to represent sounds. To use linguistic terms, all phonemes have a grapheme. Writing at this level is difficult to read.

Example: *I lik two fli a kit.* [I like to fly a kite.]

Transitional. At this level, the child knows most of the orthographic patterns of English. All sounds have letters, and for the most part, the child chooses the correct letter or combination of letters to represent sounds. Mistakes frequently occur with sounds that have several spellings (the long *a* has many spellings, and the child writes *nayborhood*). Transitional spelling is easy to read.

Example: *He is on a spaceship sershing for a krater.* [He is on a spaceship searching for a crater.]

Conventional. The child has mastered English orthography and spells almost all words correctly. The only mistakes at this level occur when the child tries to spell words new to him or her with irregular spellings. Children at this level generally recognize that a word they have spelled "doesn't look right."

Example: [The previous paragraph was, I hope, an example of conventional spelling!]

Methods of Assessing Spelling Development

In isolation: The spelling test. The traditional spelling test, during which the teacher reads words aloud and the children write them, is one way of assessing spelling development. It asks children to encode words in isolation. The words included on the test, of course, should be words that the children have been introduced to and had a chance to study (more on the selection of words for study below).

In context: Writing samples. Teachers should never rely solely on spelling tests to make judgments about the spelling development of their students. The real question is whether or not children will spell words correctly when they write. Teachers should collect samples of student work – their journals, their stories, their answers to questions – and analyze them. The teacher should look for patterns, consistent spelling choices the child makes. Which sound-symbol correspondence has the child clearly mastered? Which patterns is this child close to getting correct? For example, a teacher looks at the written work of a student and notices that he appears to think that the *c* only makes the *s* sound, and is using a *k* when a *c* is called for (*kap* for *cap*, *kan* for *can*). This assessment dictates that a series of lessons on *c* as *k* are in order.

How to Teach Spelling

Systematic Spelling Instruction

Spelling lists and tests. The traditional approach of providing a classroom of children with a list of 10–20 words to learn each week can be productive if (a) the words are appropriate and (b) other methods are used to teach spelling. Also, teachers should differentiate the number of words children are expected to learn. A reasonable expectation for some children might be only 4–5 words a week.

It is essential the words be appropriate for the children. Beware, a list of words that appears in a commercially published spelling book may or may not be right for any one group of students. What type of words should appear on spelling tests?

(1) Groups of words that have commonly occurring orthographic patterns: rimes, blends, digraphs, diphthongs, prefixes, suffixes, common root words.

(2) High-frequency words, especially those that have irregular patterns. Lists of high-frequency words include the Fry New Instant Word List or the Dolch List.

(3) Common need words: words that several children in the class have difficulty spelling correctly.

(4) Content area words: words taken from social studies and science units of study.

A variety of instructional strategies should be used to teach children to spell the words on the list.

First, when the words share an orthographic pattern, the teacher should teach direct, explicit lessons focusing on that orthographic pattern. Again, if the goal is to teach the —ate rime, the spelling list should have several words with that pattern, like mate, fate, late, hate.

Second, children should be taught how to engage in self-study of the words. It is a good idea to have a pretest so children know which words need to be studied. A simple method for self-study is the following sequence:

1. Look at the word and say it to yourself
2. Say each letter in the word to yourself
3. Close your eyes and spell the word to yourself
4. Write the word, check your spelling
5. Write the word again

Third, teachers should use multi-sensory techniques, especially for young children and those having particular difficulty. These techniques include kinesthetic approaches, like writing words in the air with large strokes; and tactile approaches, such as tracing the word on sandpaper.

Finally, teachers should select words that will facilitate direct lessons on the etymology and morphology of words. Morphological lessons focus on prefixes, suffixes, and root words. Etymology is the study of the origin and development of words. For example, a sixth grade teacher could include the following words on a spelling test: nutrition, nutrient, and nurse. All have a common origin, the Latin word nutrire, meaning to nuture.

Small group and individualized spelling instruction. Spelling lessons and tests for a classroom of students must be used in conjunction with small group and individualized spelling instruction. The results of assessment, both spelling tests and the analysis of student writing, will reveal that some children share specific needs. These children should be placed in a small group and the teacher should provide direct, explicit instruction on the orthographic pattern they need to learn. Individual intervention in spelling can be very productive. Sometimes all that is required is a 10-minute lesson in a one-on-one setting to teach a child a bothersome pattern that the child repeatedly fails to correctly spell.

Remember, the goal of small group and individualized instruction is not to achieve immediate perfection; it is to move the child through the stage of spelling development he or she is in. Consider the following:

In the pre-phonetic stage, lessons should focus on concepts about print, phonemic awareness, and then on phonics. Children need to acquire the alphabetic principle and then begin to associate the correct symbol to a sound.

In the phonetic stage, the focus is on phonics, teaching children regular, frequently occurring sound-symbol correspondences. As the child moves through this stage, lessons should include rimes, prefixes, and suffixes.

When children are transitional spellers, lessons on the morphology and etymology of words will be helpful (i.e., a lesson on the common root, *graph*, meaning *writing*). Other lessons should reveal alternative spellings for the same sound. For example, the many ways to make the long *a* sound (compare *bait, fate, hay, neighbor*).

Conventional spellers should expand their knowledge by learning highly irregular words and words for specific content areas. For example, during a unit on planets, students would learn how to spell *asteroid, satellite,* and *orbit*.

Spelling Instruction in Context

Students need opportunities to apply spelling skills they have learned with writing experiences in several curricular areas, especially social studies and science. Spelling lists at every grade level should occasionally include words from the content areas. The key is providing children many opportunities to write essays, notes, and reports in social studies and science.

Chapter 7
Content Area 7:
Reading Comprehension

Introduction

Comprehension Skills

Once again, a <u>skill</u> is something a proficient reader can do automatically. The RICA Content Specifications list the following comprehension skills:

Literal comprehension skills

Identifying the main idea when it is explicitly stated
Identifying important details
Identifying the sequence of events in a story
Identifying cause-and-effect relationships

Inferential comprehension skills

Inferring the main idea when it is not explicitly stated
Inferring details, sequence of events, and cause-and-effect relationships

Evaluative comprehension skills

Recognizing an author's bias
Detecting propaganda
Distinguishing between fact and opinion

Comprehension Strategies

<u>Strategies</u>, on the other hand, are tools that proficient readers consciously choose to better understand what they are reading. The RICA Content Specifications identify the following as comprehension strategies:

Self-monitoring. Good readers evaluate themselves and realize when they don't understand the text. Interestingly enough, less able readers rarely monitor their reading and do not alter their behavior when they don't understand what they are reading.

Rereading. This is called a "repair" strategy. A reader's self-monitoring reveals that he or she doesn't understand a text. A good reader stops and does something. The most common repair strategy is to go back and reread, usually to the previous paragraph or page. Other repair strategies include asking the teacher a question, looking up the meaning of a word in a dictionary, or taking a second look at an illustration.

Summarizing. Proficient readers can identify the main ideas of what they have read. They can retell a story or an essay in shortened form by highlighting the important elements of what they have read.

Note-taking and outlining. Note-taking and outlining are two techniques a reader could use to summarize and organize the important information in a text.

Mapping. Proficient readers can represent the significant events of a story, usually in a chronological format. To represent the structure of a story, readers can use story maps, story grammars, and story frames (all described below).

Learning logs. Learning logs are a place for children to record their thoughts about what they have read, to generate questions, speculate, or summarize.

The RICA Content Specifications require teachers to know how to assess reading comprehension and use the results of assessment to teach appropriate comprehension skills and strategies.

How to Assess Reading Comprehension

To Determine Independent, Instructional, and Frustration Reading Levels

It is important that teachers know the independent, instructional, and frustration reading levels of every student in the classroom. This information tells you, in a general sense, what level of reading material each student can comprehend. Teachers should use the graded reading passages of an informal reading inventory (IRI) to gather this information. The use of the graded reading passages on an IRI and the process of determining reading levels was described in Chapter 1. Remember, these reading levels are a function of (a) the percentage of words the child read aloud correctly and (b) the percentage of comprehension questions the child answered correctly. The comprehension questions usually will be at the literal level – asking for answers that are explicitly stated in the text.

After you have properly administered the graded reading passages of an IRI, you will know the instructional level for each of your students. This is important, because this is the reading level where instruction will work – the child's reading textbook should be at this level. Materials selected for a guided reading lesson should be at the child's instructional level (guided reading is described below). The results of this type of "placement" assessment does not reveal two things: (1) whether or not a student will be able to read a specific story or article, because the instructional level generated by an IRI is a rough estimate, and (2) whether or not the student has "higher" level comprehension skills, that is, the ability to make inferences and evaluate.

Another method of determining instructional reading level is to use the placement tests provided by the publishers of basal reading textbooks.

To Assess Comprehension Skills

All too often, teachers only assess literal comprehension. To be sure that all levels of comprehension are tested, use either QARs or Bloom's Taxonomy as a framework for creating a simple test.

Using Question-Answer Relationships (QARs)

Taphy Raphael created the QAR system to teach reading comprehension. It can also be used to assess students' mastery of all levels of comprehension skills – literal, inferential, evaluative. The QAR system places all questions that can be asked about a text into four categories on the basis of their relationship to where the answer to the question can be found:

Right there. This type of question measures literal comprehension. The answer to the question is easy to find in the text (i.e., the answer is "right there" on page 142, second paragraph, third sentence). The answer is in a single identifiable sentence. Example, from the first chapter of *Charlotte's Web* by E.B. White. Why did Mr. Arable think he should kill Wilbur? [Because he was the runt of the litter.]

Think and search. This is another type of literal comprehension question. The answer is in the text, but it is in two different parts of the text (the complete answer is not in a single sentence). Example: How do we know that Fern loves Wilbur? [On page 4, she says, "Oh, look at him! He's absolutely perfect." On page 7, she can't stop thinking about Wilbur, and answers that Wilbur is the capital city of Pennsylvania.]

Author and you. The answer is not in the text. This type of QAR asks for inferential skills. The reader needs to think about what he or she already knows, then what the author wrote, and put it together to answer the question. Example: Fern will have to feed and care for Wilbur, feeding him with a baby bottle. She is eight years old. If you have taken care of a pet, you know what a large responsibility that is. What will Fern have to do to keep Wilbur safe and well? Do you think she can do it? [Answers to this type of question will vary.]

On my own. The answer to this type of question is not in the story. You can answer the question without reading the story. Depending on the question, these can be either inferential or evaluative questions. Evaluative questions ask for students to detect bias or to distinguish fact from opinion. Example: Fern says that it is "unfair" to kill Wilbur just because he is small and weak and is the runt of the litter. Is she right? Would it have been unfair? Suppose Fern slept late, and Wilbur was killed. Would you think Mr. Arable had done a terrible thing? [Again, answers will vary.]

Teachers can assess levels of comprehension by developing a simple comprehension test using QARs. Select a story from a basal reader, and write three questions of each type. Have the students read the selection silently and answer the questions. You should have a much clearer idea of each student's ability to answer literal, inferential, and evaluative questions.

Or, You Could Use Bloom's Taxonomy

The cognitive domain of the Taxonomy of Educational Objectives, more popularly known as "Bloom's Taxonomy," can also be used to design a simple comprehension test that will assess all levels of reading comprehension skills (Benjamin Bloom, of course, was the lead author of the project that created the taxonomy). The cognitive domain has six levels: knowledge, comprehension, application, analysis, synthesis, and evaluation. Questions at the knowledge and comprehension levels measure literal comprehension; questions at the application, analysis, and synthesis levels measure inferential comprehension; and questions at the evaluation level measure evaluative comprehension skills.

The bottom line is that the only way to assess the different levels of comprehension skills (literal, inferential, and evaluative) is to ask children to answer questions at each level.

Retellings

The use of retellings has become a popular way of assessing the literal comprehension of young readers. Since many kindergarteners and first graders have limited abilities to write, comprehension skills must be assessed orally. A retelling is less threatening than the teacher firing questions at a five-year-old, a procedure that all too often resembles an interrogation rather than an appropriate primary grade assessment. After a student has read a story, the teacher asks the child to retell it.

There are two types of retellings. In an unaided retelling, the child simply is asked to retell the story (unaided retelling is also called free retelling or recall). The teacher provides no guidance. After the unaided retelling, the teacher usually proceeds with aided recall by asking the student if he or she remembers anything about a major component of the story he or she failed to mention (aided recall is also called probed recall). For example, in a retelling of Jack and the Beanstalk, if the child only talked about the ending of the story, the teacher might ask, "What happened before Jack climbed up the beanstalk?"

The teacher needs a checklist of items that a student should mention. The checklist can be organized by the literary elements (setting, characters, plot events). The teacher checks off each item if the child mentions it. Another way to organize the checklist is by the main events of the story, with supporting details listed under each main event. Again, it is important to note that retellings test literal comprehension. Unless they have been prompted by a question, children rarely make inferences or evaluate what they have read.

To Assess Reading Comprehension Strategies

The RICA Content Specifications expect teachers to model and teach strategies readers use to clarify the meaning of a text. Specifically, the Content Specifications mention self-monitoring, rereading, and summarizing. Unfortunately, it is difficult to assess these comprehension strategies because all are internal, mental operations.

Oral Think Alouds

Think alouds can be used as an assessment tool to see which students monitor their reading, reread when they don't understand something, and are able to summarize what they have read. Any selection from a basal reader or from a social studies or science textbook can be used so long as it will be challenging for the child who is reading it.

Think alouds should be done individually; the teacher works with one student. The teacher asks the student to stop at two points in time: (1) any time he is having difficulty understanding the text, and (2) at the end of a paragraph or a page. Each time the child stops, the teacher says "please tell me anything that you are thinking about now."

Again, the selection the child reads should cause some difficulty. The teacher is looking for the following things:

Does the child self-monitor? That is, does the student note when he or she is having difficulty (by saying things like, "this is hard," or "I don't get what's going on"). Does the student note when she or he is not having difficulty ("this is easy," or the child makes a reasonable inference or speculation).

When in trouble, does the child select a repair strategy, like re-reading? The child would say something like "I better go back and read this paragraph again."

Does the child generate questions the text will likely answer? The child might say, "I don't think Mr. Arable will kill the pig." Or, "I wonder how Fern will stop her father if he decides to kill Wilber."

Does the child accurately summarize what he or she has read? The child would say something like "Well, in that chapter we learned how Fern saved Wilbur and he became her pet."

Written Assessments of Reading Comprehension Strategies

Note-taking, outlining, mapping, and learning logs all can be used to assess reading comprehension strategies. For assessment, the teacher would ask students to read something and, while reading, either take notes, make an outline, draw a story map, or keep a learning log.

The learning log can become the written version of the oral think aloud process described in the previous section. Again, students are told to stop reading whenever they have difficulty and at certain predetermined points in the selection (end of a paragraph, end of page). The student would write down in the log what he or she is thinking. One alternative is to ask the students to write down questions they think will be answered by the rest of the selection. Proficient readers will write questions that flow logically from what has been read. Less able readers tend to write questions that have <u>already</u> been answered in the text.

How to Teach Reading Comprehension

Research shows that comprehension skills and strategies can be taught. To teach comprehension, teachers should do three things:

(1) Facilitate comprehension by designing and implementing lessons that will help children better comprehend a specific selection, like a story in a reading textbook.

(2) Teach reading comprehension skills (literal, inferential, evaluative) and reading comprehension strategies so that children will be able to read more proficiently on their own.

(3) Teach children how to become more proficient when they read specific types of texts, like social studies and science textbooks. This will be covered in Chapter 9, Content-Area Literacy.

Facilitating Comprehension of a Specific Selection
(Like a Story in a Reader)

Before Children Read

Before they read, teachers should (1) help children activate their background knowledge of the topic they are reading about and (2) teach the meanings of difficult words in the selection.

Direct instruction to activate background knowledge: KWL and PreP. Children will have a better chance of understanding what they are about to read if their teacher helps them call to mind what they know about the topic of the selection. In simple words, we don't know all that we know. This is called "activating background knowledge."

The use of <u>KWL</u> charts has become a popular way of helping children activate their background knowledge. KWL charts help students activate, think about, and organize their prior knowledge. The teacher prepares a chart with three columns, *K*, *W*, and *L*. Let's assume a small group of children are about to read a story about penguins. The teacher asks the children "What do you *know* about penguins?" and records their responses under the *K*. Then the teacher asks "What would you like to *learn* about penguins?" and records the students' responses under the *L*. After the story has been read, the final column is completed as they teacher asks "What have we learned about penguins?"

PreP, the Prereading Plan, is another way teachers can help their children call to mind what they know about a topic. PreP is a structured discussion with three steps:

(1) Associations. The teachers says, "Tell me anything you think of when you hear the word *penguins*." The teacher records these initial associations.

(2) Reflections on the Associations. The teacher asks some of the students who responded, "What made you think of (whatever the child said about penguins)? Often, many new associations come forth during this part of the discussion.

(3) Organizing Associations. The teacher then asks, "Do any of you have new or different ideas or thoughts about *penguins*? Many children will, at this point, recall additional information they know about the topic.

Teaching the meanings of difficult words. This will be covered in a separate chapter on vocabulary instruction, Chapter 12.

Guided Reading

Unfortunately, most elementary teachers attempt to teach comprehension through a single activity. A small group of children read a story in their basal reader either silently or orally (typically, one child reads aloud at a time). Every once in a while, usually at the end of a page, the teacher asks questions provided in the teachers' edition of the reader. This process tests comprehension to some degree, by showing which children understand what is happening in the story, but unless the teacher does more of the ask-read-ask process, it does nothing to teach comprehension and make children better readers.

Guided reading, an instructional format developed in New Zealand, provides an alternative to the standard "read-ask-read-ask" lesson format. Guided reading has become very popular in the United States.

It is difficult to define precisely what guided reading is for two reasons. First, reading specialists and teachers have developed their own models, each with variations. Second, not all guided reading lessons follow the same format. Here are the essential features of guided reading:

* Guided reading lessons are planned for a small group of children, all of whom have the same instructional reading levels. This is essential, all the children must read at the same level.

* Usually, the selections are written at a level that challenges the children to the degree that they would have some difficulty reading the selection on their own. Note, though, that depending on the lesson, the teacher may select a story the children can read easily (if the teacher wants to work on difficult comprehension skills or strategies such as inferencing or self-monitoring). Many publishers produce small books specially designed for guided reading lessons. Guided reading lessons can also be done with stories in basal readers.

* The teacher's goal is to assist children so they can become independent readers. The focus is helping children become proficient in (a) word identification and (b) the reading comprehension strategies of predicting, confirming, and self-correcting.

* Children in a class will be grouped and regrouped as the year progresses, depending on their path of development.

More specifically, a guided reading lesson looks like this:

Before reading. The teacher introduces the story. This may mean talking about one or two words that the children will likely have not seen before.

A popular activity many teachers choose to introduce a story is a "picture talk;" the story is previewed as the teacher looks at the illustrations with the children.

The teacher may work on a comprehension strategy, like predicting. For example, the teacher could ask children to read the title and look at the first picture and predict what the story will be about.

During reading. Usually, the children read the story silently. Sometimes, though, the teacher may want to read a part of the story aloud if that part will be the focus of attention. For example, a teacher may want to model the strategy of confirming. The teacher would read aloud and think aloud, stopping at some point to say, "I forgot why Mr. and Mrs. Mallard decided to leave the island; I think it was because it wasn't safe. Let's go back and see if I am right."

Sometimes, the teacher will pull a child aside and listen to him or her read aloud, asking the child to think aloud about what he or she is reading. The teacher is ready to answer questions children ask.

After reading. There are many possibilities here. The teacher could teach a mini-lesson on a reading strategy, like summarizing or confirming. For summarizing, children might be asked to retell the story in only three or four sentences. If children made predictions at some point while reading, these should be confirmed.

Many times there will be a "language play" mini-lesson. For language play, the teacher looks at the story for something that would serve as the substance for a lesson on phonics, other word identification, punctuation, or vocabulary. For example, the story

<u>Make Way for Ducklings</u> by Robert McClossky could generate a lesson on two different spellings of the long *a* sound, *a* /consonant/silent *e* (as in *make*) and *ay* as in *way*.

Other "after reading" activities could include a simple discussion of the story or a writing or art project based on the story. Many times the teacher will ask the children to reread the story, either to a partner or independently.

Strategies and Skills Instruction

Strategy Instruction: Reciprocal Teaching

Reading strategies, once again, include self-monitoring, repair strategies (like clarifying and rereading), predicting, confirming, and summarizing. Reciprocal Teaching is an instructional process for teaching strategies. Research has shown that teachers who consistently use reciprocal teaching will help their students become better at reading comprehension.

Reciprocal teaching was developed to teach four strategies: <u>Generating</u> questions, <u>summarizing</u>, <u>clarifying</u> (word meanings and confusing text), and <u>predicting</u> what might appear in the next paragraph. The teacher (1) explains how the strategy should be used, (2) models its use, usually through a think aloud, and (3) helps children use the strategy independently.

Reciprocal teaching lessons are planned for a small group of students. The teacher decides which strategy will be the focus of the lesson. When children become more proficient, a lesson may work on two or more strategies.

Everyone has a copy of the selection, which usually is read paragraph by paragraph. The teacher tells the children which strategy they will be working on and how it helps one become a better reader. The paragraph is read by the teacher and the children, sometimes silently, sometimes orally. The teacher models the use of the strategy. For example, the teacher may pretend to be confused and say "I am not sure why Sally wants to sell her computer. I am going to reread the last two paragraphs" or "I don't know what a *wardrobe* is, I better look it up in the dictionary."

Gradually, the teacher does less and less. The students assume the roles he or she was playing. The teacher, as students take over, helps the students master the strategies by asking questions, resolving misunderstandings, and, if necessary, re-modeling the use of the strategy.

Skills Instruction: Using Question-Answer Relationships (QARs) to Teach Inferential and Evaluative Comprehension

Children having difficulty in reading typically have very poorly developed inferential and evaluative comprehension skills. Usually they cannot answer inferential and evaluative comprehension questions because they treat every question as if it were a literal one, with an answer clearly stated in the text. One key to mastering inferential and evaluative questions is being able to distinguish different types of comprehension questions. Otherwise, children will waste a great deal of time trying to find the answers to inferential and evaluative questions when, in fact, the answers are not stated clearly in the text.

Lessons based on QARs will help children make the connection between question type and the information sources necessary and available for answering questions. The four types of QARs were described previously in this chapter. Once again, they are:

Right there – the answer to the question is in the text in a single identifiable sentence.

Think and search – the answer is in the text, but it is in two different parts of the text (the complete answer is not in a single sentence).

Author and you – the answer is not in the text. You need to think about what you already know, what the author said, and put it together.

On my own – the answer is not in the story. You can answer the question without reading the story.

The ultimate goal of QAR lessons is to get children to be able to look at a question and say, "that is an author and you question, I don't need to look for an answer in the text, I just need to think and write." Lessons focus on helping children identify and classify questions. A group of children reads a story in the basal reader. The teacher and the students look at a set of questions, like those provided in the teachers' edition, and classify each question before trying to answer it.

At first, teachers may want to work on just distinguishing *right there* and *think and search* questions since both do have answer sources in the text. Next, the teacher could help children distinguish the two types of questions that do not have answers in the text, *author and you* and *on my own* questions.

Better Comprehension Through Understanding Story Structure: Story Maps, Story Grammars and Story Frames

So far, we have looked at three ways teachers can help their students better comprehend what they have read: (1) by facilitating comprehension before, during, and after students read a specific selection, (2) by teaching comprehension strategies through reciprocal teaching, and (3) by teaching comprehension skills through QARs. Teachers should also teach their students to use the structure of stories to read more proficiently.

When students develop a sense of how stories are formed they will be able to store information more efficiently, better remember details from all parts of a story, and recall story details with greater accuracy. Students can be taught to attend to story structure through story maps, story grammars, and story frames.

For story maps, story grammars, and story frames, teachers first provide complete models and use the models to discuss the story. Then, the teacher provides "skeletal" maps, grammars, and frames. Students complete these during and after they read, with help from the teacher. Next, students are challenged to complete the skeletal maps, grammars, and frames on their own. Finally, older students should be able to create their own maps, grammars, and frames.

Story mapping. Story maps represent stories in a visual diagram by highlighting certain elements of the story. Making a story map helps students think about the structure of a story and how things relate to each other.

In some story maps the name of the story is placed in a circle in the center of the diagram and characters, events, and locations are placed in satellite position around the title. Lines show relationships. Other story maps actually look like things (fish, spider webs, etc.). The goal is to organize story information in graphic shapes like fish and fishbones (cause-and-effect relationships), or spider webs (details organized under identified sub topics, branched away from the center of the web).

The simplest story map would look like this:

Title

Beginning   Middle   End

Children would list story events under the appropriate section.

Story grammars. A story grammar is an outline. A common template for a story grammar would look like this:

Setting

Problem
The Goal

      Event 1
      Event 2
      Event 3

Resolution

Story frames. Story frames are the simplest story structure device to complete; students just fill in the blanks. For example:

Title: _____

In this story, the problem starts when _____
After that _____

Next, _____
Then, _____

The problem is finally solved when _____
The story ends when _____

Improving Fluency

Reading fluency refers to how fast and with how much expression a person uses when reading aloud. Fluent readers read at an appropriate pace and with vocalizing expressions so that listeners can understand what is happening in the story without difficulty. Several things can inhibit reading fluency including: poorly developed decoding skills, a lack of sight word knowledge, and a failure to properly "chunk" text phrasing. All good readers know to pause after a comma and when they come to the end of a sentence. In addition, fluent readers understand the text as they read orally. It is apparent.

Assessing fluency is relatively easy. It requires a tape recorder and tapes of children reading aloud. There are precise formulas for determining if a child at any grade level is reading fast enough. Most teachers, however, can tell who among their students reads at an appropriate pace with good expression and who struggles through oral reading experiences.

There are many instructional activities teachers can select to improve reading fluency. First, many fluency problems end when students have increased their sight vocabularies and improved their decoding skills. One technique that helps fluency is repeated readings. Students read the same, short block of text over and over again. Poems work well for repeated readings. The student reads the text aloud several times. The student should read it to herself, to classmates, to parents, and to the teacher. In one model of repeated reading, the student is encouraged to time herself to see how much faster each reading becomes.

In assisted reading, children read with a classmate. This is also called buddy reading, dyad reading, or paired reading. The two children read the same text aloud together, providing support for each other. This mutual support helps students read faster and with better expression.

Choral reading takes place when two or more people read aloud. Usually, choral reading involves many children (sometimes the entire class). Choral reading improves fluency because the less able readers are able to hear fluent models and they can "jump on board" as their more able classmates read at a brisk pace.

In reader's theater presentations, the actors read their scripts. Children can dramatize poems, picture book stories, and chapters from novels through reader's theater. In a reader's theater production, children have a chance to repeatedly practice reading aloud their parts. These repeated readings allow students to increase the pace of their oral reading.

Chapter 8
Content Area 8:
Literary Response and Analysis

Introduction

"Literary response and analysis," the RICA Content Specifications state, "refer to a process in which students extend their understanding and appreciation of significant literary works representing a wide range of genres, perspectives, eras, and cultures." Children should have opportunities to respond to literature orally and in writing. Teachers should ask open-ended questions to allow their students to respond freely to the books they have read (i.e., "Tell me the first thing that comes to your mind when you think of Out of the Dust."). Teachers should also ask more direct questions to encourage response (for example, "Do you know any people who remind you of Billie Jo?").

Literary analysis focuses on the literary elements: character, setting, plot, theme, mood, style. Teachers should help students see how writers use figurative language, like similes and metaphors, in novels and poetry. Students also should be asked to see how books reflect the perspectives of the time and place when they were written.

The RICA Content Specifications call for teachers to have a well-planned literature program. Teachers are responsible for selecting high quality literature for their students to read. Most important, the expectation is that teachers "provide explicit instruction and guided practice in responding to literature and analyzing literary text structures and elements." Thus, we are talking about more than merely asking children to check out a book from the school or classroom library, read it, and then fill out some type of book report form.

How to Assess Literary Response and Analysis

Students Read and Teacher Reads Aloud

Teachers should assess literary understanding by asking students to respond to and analyze (a) books that children have read themselves and (b) books that the teacher reads aloud.

Oral and Written

Teachers evaluate students' response and analysis through both oral and written assessments. For our younger students especially, it is important that assessment be done orally. Many children will have thoughts and feelings about books they cannot express in writing.

Free and Focused

It is important that the assessment of literary understanding be both free and focused. Free response requires the use of open-ended prompts like:

> Who has something they would like to say about The Polar Express by Chris Van Allsburg?

> Write anything you want about The Polar Express.

Focused prompts tend to use the literary elements as a basis for questions. For example:

> How are Alyce in The Midwife's Apprentice by Karen Cushman and Billie Jo in Out of the Dust by Karen Hesse alike? How are they different? (Question based on character.)

> We have read two books by Margaret Wise Brown and two books by Dr. Seuss. Do these authors tell their stories the same way? (Question based on style.)

Analysis of Results

The RICA Content Specifications provide a portrait of what elementary students should demonstrate in the area of literary understanding. As teachers analyze oral and written responses they should see students:

Incorporate literary elements into their analysis of books. Some examples: Do students focus on the characters in a story? Do they mention specific incidents that help the reader understand a character? Do children ever talk or write about the setting of the story? Do they notice how the story's time and place influences what is happening? Do students understand the plot device of conflict? Can they identify the point in a story when the plot's central conflict is resolved?

Make connections to the literature they read. Examples: Do children talk or write about similar characters or settings in two different books? When asked, can students link a book to their own lives by, for instance, mentioning a personal challenge that was similar to one faced by a character in a book?

Provide evidence from a text to support their responses. Finally, are children able to cite specific events or descriptions in a story to support the perspectives they have stated or written? For example, after a child reads Holes by Louis Sachar, she writes "Stanley grew up during the story." Can this student cite an example of how Stanley changed during his experience at Camp Green Lake?

Participation Checklists

Finally, some teachers use checklists to evaluate students as they participate in literature-related activities. The results of such a checklist can be compared over the course of the school year. A checklist might include items like:

Promptly selects a new book after finishing another

Maintains an accurate log of all books read

Listens attentively during discussions of books

Comments reflect a thorough understanding of the book

Asks questions that challenge perspectives of other students

Comments about each of the following during a discussion:
Character
Setting
Plot
Theme
Style
Mood

How to Teach Literary Response and Analysis

Responding to Literature

To provide a setting in which children can respond to literature, the RICA Content Specifications ask that teachers do teach with the following criteria in mind.

Select Literature from a Wide Range of Eras, Perspectives, and Cultures

The first job of the teacher is to ensure that students are exposed to a variety of high-quality books. Some of these books will be read aloud by the teacher; others will be read by the children, either independently or in small groups. To achieve the range of depth of literary response and analysis called for by the RICA Content Specifications, children must work with good books. Perhaps the most useful selection tool is a document produced by the California Department of Education, Recommended Readings in Literature, Kindergarten through Grade Eight. Now in its third edition, this booklet recommends and annotates hundreds of good children's books. Special attention is given to books written by and about California's ethnic minority groups.

Teachers should be aware of books that have won awards. All classrooms should shelve books that have won the two most prestigious awards: the Newbery and Caldecott Medal winners, which are each given annually by the American Library Association. The

Newbery Medal is awarded to the best children's book written by an American author (usually a novel). The Caldecott Medal is given to the best illustrated American picture book. Lists of these award-winning books and illustrators can be located in libraries, your college reading and children's literature textbooks, and online at (need web site).

Provide Students with Frequent Opportunities to Listen to and Read High-Quality Literature for Different Purposes

Effective teachers select a variety of instructional models to provide meaningful experiences with literature. It is important to note, however, that in a balanced approach to reading, experiences with literature must be used in conjunction with direct, explicit lessons in the other RICA Content Areas. In the type of classroom described by the RICA Content Specifications, literature experiences are a part of the reading program, not the entire reading program.

In the core book approach, each member of a class has a copy of an important work in children's literature. All students read the book, or listen to their teacher read it, and complete a variety of assignments which encourage response and analysis. Literature units expose children to a variety of good books that share a common element, which may be the same author, theme, or genre (a type of book). All classrooms need time when children can read books they have selected. Some teachers expand this self-selected, self-paced component into a model called readers workshop. Also, during literature study groups, a small group of children all read, respond, and analyze the same book. (These groups are also called grand conversation groups or book clubs.)

Use Instructional Approaches That Help Students Apply Comprehension Strategies When Reading Literature and Develop Students' Ability to Respond to It

The RICA Content Specifications mention three specific instructional approaches to help students analyze and respond to literature. Guided reading was described in the previous chapter. The Guided Reading format can be used to develop literary response. During a Guided Reading lesson, the teacher should seize opportunities to encourage children to talk about what they have read. Again, the teachers' questions should be a mixture of open-ended prompts to stimulate free response and focused questions to summon responses that identify specific characters, events, themes, or writing styles.

Asking students to keep reading logs or journals is essential. Students should keep records of and write about books they have read. Teachers should use a variety of prompts to stimulate written response. In addition to the open-ended and focused questions mentioned several times in this chapter, some teachers use "quotes and notes." Each child selects a sentence from a book he has read, copies it verbatim in his or her journal, and then writes a comment about the quote underneath it. In "double-entry journals," each child writes a comment about a book and then leaves space for the teacher or another student to write a reply.

Discussions about literature should take place on a regular basis. The role of the teacher varies during these discussions. Usually the goal of the teacher is to facilitate, not dominate any discussion. The more the teacher prompts individual children to respond to the literature, the better. When the teacher wants to focus oral response on a specific part of a book, like a character, then she must ask more focused questions.

Analyzing Literature

Describing and Analyzing Story Elements

At the center of instruction related to the analysis of the literature are the literary elements. Teachers should directly teach about each element. For example, older students should know the functions of setting in a story: to clarify conflict, serve as the antagonist, amplify character, establish mood, serve as a symbol. The literary elements also should serve as the basis for many of the questions teachers ask children about the books they have read. Below is a brief summary of the literary elements:

Character. In children's literature, characters usually are people. Some children's books have animals, plants, or inanimate things as characters (like a stuffed animal, for example). Older students should be able to identify the protagonist(s) and antagonist(s) in a novel. The protagonist is the main character of the story, or in more literary terms, the character who "pushes toward" something. In colloquial terms the antagonist is the "bad guy," the character who pushes against the protagonist and tries to block him from achieving his goal.

Plot. The sequence of events in a story is its plot. Many novels and plays written in English follow a plot structure that includes an introduction; rising action during which the reader is introduced to conflict or complication; a climax when the conflict is resolved; and then falling action to wrap things up (called the denouement). Some stories break the normal flow of events with flashbacks and flashforwards, which present events out of chronological order.

Setting. Teachers should help students understand that the setting of a book is both the time and the place of the story. Role settings in a story can be said to serve as a backdrop or be integral to the story, or apply somewhere in between. A story with a backdrop setting has a vaguely defined setting and could take place in a number of places or times (like most fairy tales). Integral settings are fully described and the story can only take place in that time and in that place (like most historical fiction).

Mood, theme, and **style** are discussed in subsequent sections of this chapter.

Determining Mood and Theme

Elementary school children will have difficulty in identifying and describing a story's mood and theme. Mood is the feeling you have when you are reading the story, which can be spooky, comforting, majestic, etc. In picture books, illustrations convey the mood. Scary moods usually are represented with dark colors, with things that are literally or figuratively cloaked or are only partially revealed. Joy and happiness typically are established with lots of light and bright colors. In novels, authors create mood by using descriptive words. A mood of suspense and impending danger can be created by foreshadowing (giving the reader a hint of the trouble ahead).

A story's theme is its important message, usually a comment about the human condition. Theme can be clearly stated (an explicit theme) or the reader must infer it (an implicit theme). For example, the Newbery-winning book <u>Out of the Dust</u> has an explicit theme. The author Karen Hesse states "you can stay in one place and still grow." On the other hand, readers must infer the theme of "the grass isn't always greener on the other side of the fence" in <u>The Little House</u> by Laura Ingalls Wilder. Even our youngest students can discern a book's central message if they taught what to look for and how to look for it.

Analyzing the Use of Figurative Language

Style is the way authors use words and illustrators use visual images. It is not the "what" of the story, it is <u>how the story is told</u>. Words have both a literal meaning and a figurative meaning. Figurative language is the use of words in a non-literal way, giving them meaning beyond their everyday definition – providing an extra dimension to the meaning of the word. Some examples of figurative language are:

<u>Hyperbole</u>. An exaggerated comparison. Example: "scared to death."

<u>Metaphor</u>. A metaphor is an implied comparison. Example: "The road was a river of moonlight."

<u>Personification</u>. Giving human traits to non-human beings or inanimate objects. Example: "The crickets sang in the grasses. They sang the song of summer's ending."

<u>Simile</u>. This is one of the simplest figurative devices. A simile is a stated comparison between unlike things using the words *like* or *as*. Example: "He was as big as a house."

<u>Symbol</u>. A person, object, situation, or action that operates on two levels of meaning – the literal and the symbolic. Example: in <u>The Polar Express</u>, the small bell is a symbol for the true meaning of Christmas.

Recognizing Features of Literary Genres

Genres are categories or types of stories. The RICA Content Specifications call for teachers to teach children how to recognize the features of different literary genres. This can be done first by exposing children to several examples of a particular genre and then, through direct instruction, listing their common elements. The following genres cover most children's books:

Traditional literature. These are stories that have their origins in oral storytelling and have survived through generations. Examples of folktales are cumulative tales (such as The House that Jack Built), pourquoi tales (which explain a natural phenomena, such as Why Mosquitos Buzz in People's Ears by Verna Aardema), trickster tales (B'rer Rabbit from Uncle Remus) and fairy tales (stories full of enchantment and magic). Traditional literature also includes tall tales (with much exaggeration), fables (which teach a lesson), and myths (which people created to explain the world around them).

Modern fantasy. Modern fantasy includes those stories that are magical or play with the laws of nature and have known authors. This includes animal fantasy, with beasts that can talk; stories with toys and dolls that act like people; and stories with tiny humans.

High fantasy. This is a popular type of modern fantasy for older children. High fantasy has a struggle between good and evil set in a fantastic world. The hero or heroine of the story usually goes on a quest of some sort. Examples include The Lion, the Witch, and the Wardrobe by C.S. Lewis and the Harry Potter books by J.K. Rowling.

Science fiction. This is a type of modern fantasy similar to high fantasy with one important difference, the story features some "improved" or "futuristic" technology. Science fiction is the genre of time machines, spaceships that travel at the speed of light, and holographic worlds.

Contemporary realistic fiction. These are stories that take place in the present day in the real world. These stories can be humorous or quite serious. Examples include the Ramona Quimby books by Beverly Cleary and recent Newbery winners such as Walk Two Moons by Sharon Creech and Missing May by Cynthia Rylant.

Historical fiction. Historical fiction includes realistic stories that are set in the past. Good historical fiction makes the past come alive to young readers. Examples: Roll of Thunder, Hear My Cry by Mildred Taylor and Island of the Blue Dolphins by Scott O'Dell.

Biography. Biographies are information books that tell the story of a real person's life. There are excellent picture book biographies written for young readers (popularized by the author Diane Stanley).

Informational books. Once called "nonfiction," informational books should present accurate information about something. These books, of course, are not stories. There are information books written for children about virtually any topic you can imagine. The style of informational books is different from fiction, and places special demands on the young reader (this will be discussed in the next chapter on content-area reading).

Analyzing Ways in Which a Literary Work Reflects the Traditions and Perspectives of a Particular People or Time

Literature can provide considerable insight about people who lived in the past and the many different cultural groups who live today. Literature has the potential to give us perspectives unlike our own. First, teachers must select books that accurately portray the way people may have viewed events of the past. In Roll of Thunder, Hear My Cry, Mildred Taylor provides young readers with an African-American view of life in the segregated Southern United States in the 1930s. Laura Ingalls grew up on the Great Plains in the late 19th century. Students can analyze her books to see how settlers dealt with the challenges of day-to-day living and see the harsh and stereotypical attitudes European Americans had toward Native Americans at that time. To provide balanced multiple views of people other than European or American whites, teachers must share authentic books written by and for African American, Native American, Hispanic American, Asian American, and international authors and illustrators.

What teachers must do to accomplish this goal is make a character's perspective the focus of a lesson. This requires readers to look beyond the entertainment of the story to find specific passages that reveal the attitudes of different people in a certain time and place.

Chapter 9
Content Area 9:
Content-Area Literacy

Introduction

Definitions

The RICA Content Specifications state that "Content-area literacy refers to the ability to learn through reading." The content areas of grade school, middle school and high school curricula include social studies, science, mathematics, health, and the study of the visual and performing arts (e.g., the history of painting; rather than how to paint). For the most part, however, content-area reading and writing focuses on social studies and science. Most content-area reading and writing assignments focus on content learned in the social studies or science content areas. Students who are effective content-area readers, however, also can read and understand information located in encyclopedias, almanacs, and on Internet web sites.

Elementary school children spend most of their time reading stories, which are examples of narrative text. Social studies and science textbooks, encyclopedias, and most Internet sites are examples of expository text. The purpose of an expository text is to inform the reader. Some elementary school children find reading expository texts to be a significant challenge.

Nonfiction books are another example of expository text. Today, most professionals in the field use the descriptor "information book" rather than nonfiction to recognize works that provide content knowledge.

Expository Text Structures

In Chapter 7 on Comprehension you read that many stories are written to follow a predictable pattern, and that teachers can use story grammars, story maps, and story frames to help children understand these patterns. Likewise, most social studies textbooks, science textbooks, and encyclopedia entries are written in standard patterns or structures. These expository text structures include:

Cause and effect. This structure is common in science textbooks where the author is showing that some phenomena are the result of some other phenomena. For example, this structure can occur in social studies textbooks when the author explains why an historical event occurred.

Problem and solution. In this type of expository text structure, the author presents a problem and then explains or provides information for the student to explain.

Comparison/contrast. In this structure, the writer examines the similarities and differences among two or more historical figures, events, or phenomena.

Sequence. The author lists items or events in numerical or chronological order.

Description. The author describes a topic by listing characteristics or features.

Teachers can use these text structures for three purposes: (1) to create an advance organizer for students to examine before they read, (2) to create a study guide to help students understand the important points of a selection during and after they read, and (3) to assess the content-area reading comprehension of students.

Students who have repeated experiences in working with expository text structures will use their knowledge of structures to become more efficient readers of content-area texts. Readers can use the author's organizational structure to make predictions about what information a chapter in a social studies or science textbook will present, to clarify information that seems contradictory, and to summarize the key points of a chapter by creating an outline or concept map based on the text structure and information the text provides.

Appendix G shows diagrams of these expository text structures.

How to Assess Content-Area Literacy

CLOZE

A CLOZE test can be used to determine whether or not a student can comprehend a specific text. CLOZE can be used with basal readers, picture books, and novels. I mention it here because it is excellent tool for teachers who want to decide whether or not a child can read his or her grade-level social studies or science textbook. It is difficult to use CLOZE with texts written below the second grade level because there aren't enough words in a chapter to create a CLOZE passage. A CLOZE test will tell you if the text is at the child's independent, instructional, or frustration reading level.

CLOZE is short for "closure." Here is how it works. Let us say, for example, that a fourth grade teacher wants to determine who among his students will have difficulty with the fourth grade science textbook. The teacher would choose a chapter in the middle of the textbook and select a passage of at least 275 words, preferably at the beginning of a chapter. It is important that the children have not read the passage before the CLOZE test. Working on a word processor or with a photocopy of the pages in the passage, the teacher deletes every fifth word, starting with the second sentence. There should be 50 blanks. The passage should conclude with a complete sentence.

The teacher would explain the CLOZE test format to the child. The child reads the passage once without doing anything. Then, he or she reads the passage and attempts to write in the missing words in the blanks created by the teacher. To score the CLOZE, the teacher calculates how many of the missing words the child was able to provide. Count as correct only exact replacements.

Authorities do not agree on the standards for determining independent, instructional, and frustration levels for CLOZE texts. The following, however, is fairly standard:

Independent reading level. The student provided over 60% of the missing words. This is good! The student will be able to read the textbook with little assistance from the teacher.

Instructional reading level. The student provided between 40% and 60% of the missing words. This is okay! The student will be able to read the text if the teacher plans effective content-area reading lessons, develops a pre-reading guide, or provides study guides to help the student understand the information presented.

Frustration reading level. The student provided fewer than 40% of the missing words. This result must be taken seriously. It means the student will have difficulty with the textbook even if the teacher provides a great deal of assistance. Teachers will need to find other ways to help the child acquire the information the text presents (easier books, charts and diagrams, audiovisual resources, peer tutors, or text structure organizers).

Using Text Structures

Teachers can use pattern guides to assess student comprehension of a content-area text. The teacher provides a "skeleton" and the students complete the missing parts. For example, take another look at Appendix G. The Venn diagram is a good way to show a comparison. A test for a science textbook chapter on the planet Mars might use a Venn diagram; one circle for Earth, the other for Mars. Students would be challenged to list three things unique to Earth (abundance of water), three things the planets share (polar caps), and three things unique to Mars (atmosphere almost entirely carbon dioxide).

Multi-Level Questions

In Chapter 7, I described how to use the QAR system to create simple tests of a child's mastery of comprehension skills, especially the "higher order" skills of inference and evaluation. Teachers should use the QAR hierarchy with social studies and science textbooks to assess their students' ability to answer all types of questions. Again, it is essential to see if students can answer the think and search, author and you, and on my own type of questions. Once again, Bloom's Taxonomy can also be used to design a simple test of all levels of reading comprehension.

Teacher Observation/Anecdotal Records

Teachers can gather useful data about the content-area reading performance of their students by simply observing their behavior and taking notes. For example, when students are asked to read in their science textbook and retrieve information by completing a chart, a teacher should note who completes the task easily and who struggles. Likewise, if a student tries to find information in an encyclopedia and is unable to use guide words to locate the appropriate entry, the teacher should make a note of that. Over the course of time, these informal notes, begin "to add up" and can be used to support your conclusions. If, for example, you think that Fred has difficulty reading his social studies textbook, then it helps if you have anecdotal notes from September 11, October 2 , and October 16 verifying that conclusion.

Readability of Texts

One other evaluation concept needs to be explained here. Readability is a measure of the difficulty of a text. Several readability formulas exist and teachers can use them to determine if a child can read a specific book (assuming you know the child's independent reading level). Readability formulas are applied to a passage from a textbook or an information book. These formulas measure the semantic difficulty of a text by calculating word length and the number of syllables in the passage and the syntactic difficulty of the text by calculating the number of words in sentences. Two well-known readability formulas are the Fry Readability Graph and the Raygor Readability Estimate.

Your reading methods text will explain how to administer a readability formula. There have always been many questions about the validity of these formulas. For one thing, they don't take into account the quality of the text's writing. Nor do they measure a student's interest in the topic the text addresses. It is always easier to read something if it is well written and we are interested in the information presented. Finally, the utility of readability formulas is diminished by the time it takes the teacher to use them.

Once again, if a teacher has determined a child's independent, instructional, and frustration reading levels through an IRI, then a readability formula would tell the teacher how a textbook or an information book from the library "fits" a child's reading ability.

How to Teach Content-Area Literacy

There are five things teachers should do to improve the content-area reading comprehension of their students: (1) use pattern guides before, during, and after children read, (2) design and implement effective content-area reading lessons when students are asked to read their social studies or science textbooks, (3) teach students to use expository text structures as a tool to predict, clarify, and summarize, (4) help children become effective at reading for different purposes (skimming, scanning, in-depth), and (5) teach children study skills to locate and retrieve information from reference materials.

Pattern Guides

The instructional strategies covered in Chapter 7 on Comprehension are, for the most part, the same ones teachers should use when students read content-area texts. The use of pattern guides, designed on the basis of a text's structure, can only be used with content-area materials (remember, though, their use is similar to the use of story grammars, story frames, and story maps for narrative text).

A pattern guide is a diagram, chart, or outline based on the text's structure (once again, take a look at Appendix G). There are two types of pattern guides. A **graphic organizer** is used before students read and is prepared by the teacher. It provides students with an overview of what they will read, usually for an entire chapter in a social studies or science textbook. A well-designed graphic organizer presents the key points of a chapter in an easy-to-read format. It is, in fact, a simple outline of the chapter (graphic organizers also are called "structured overviews").

When the teacher prepares a "skeletal" guide and the students complete it during or after they read, then the pattern guide becomes a **study guide**. The purpose of a study guide is to highlight the most important information in a chapter. Study guides based on the text's structure are particularly effective because they are allow students to use the text's structure to find the missing information. Not all study guides, however, are pattern guides. Some study guides are simply a list of questions; others are constructed using a format other than the text's structure (there will be more on study guides later in this chapter).

Content-Area Reading Lesson

Effective teachers help their students comprehend content-area reading material through well-designed content-area reading lessons. This type of lesson is used with social studies and science textbooks. Content-area lessons can be prepared for one page, several pages, or an entire chapter of a textbook. For purposes of our discussion, we will assume lessons prepared for a single chapter in a social studies or science textbook. The lesson will have elements that occur before students read, during the time they read, and after the children have finished reading.

Before Reading

Before students read, teachers should (1) help students activate their background knowledge of the topics covered in the text, (2) build students' vocabularies by teaching them the definitions of unfamiliar words in the text, (3) link the content of the text to what children have learned previously, and (4) preview the important information students will learn when they read.

Activate background knowledge. We covered two instructional strategies for activating background knowledge in Chapter 7: KWL and PreP. Either can be used with content-area texts.

Build vocabulary. This will be covered in the chapter on vocabulary instruction, Chapter 12.

Link to what students learned previously. This instructional component typically would not be used with a lesson based on a story in a basal reader because each story usually is unrelated to the stories before and after it. Chapters in a social studies or science textbook, however, usually <u>are</u> related to each other. In fact, in many instances students will be able to better understand the information presented in one chapter if they review what they have learned previously. For example, a chapter on the habitats of amphibians may be preceded by a chapter on the anatomy of amphibians. Unless students recall the unique aspects of amphibians' bodies, they won't understand why they live where they do. There are many ways to link information students will be expected to learn to what they have learned previously:

* <u>Review of a KWL chart, a data retrieval chart, or a summary chart</u>. If the class completed a KWL chart on the material they learned previously, the chart could be re-examined. Data retrieval charts and summary charts will be described later in this chapter. They could be used to review the material students read the day before a content-area reading lesson.

* <u>Reread</u>. Another easy way to review information that was presented in a previous chapter of a social studies or science text is to take a second look at that chapter. In other words, before reading Chapter 4, the teacher will have the students open their textbooks to Chapter 3. Together, the class again will look at illustrations and discuss major chapter headings. Students might also be asked to reread a summary of the chapter.

Preview what students will read. Most students will find it easier to understand the information presented in a chapter of a textbook if the teacher highlights the important information they will encounter. One effective technique to accomplish this is preparing and presenting a <u>graphic organizer</u>. A graphic organizer is an outline of a chapter based on the chapter's text structure or a graphic map that identifies major concepts and topics. A simple way to preview what students will read is through a <u>summary chart</u>. A summary chart is a list of sentences, usually no more than five, stating the key points of a chapter. For example, a teacher prepared this chart to preview a chapter about the functions of California missions:

Summary Chart – What Happened at the Missions

The missions were:
* Churches – To convert the natives to Christianity
* Forts – To defend Spain's claim to California
* Farms – To produce food for people at the mission
* Factories – To produce things needed at the mission

During/After the Reading Experience

Reading the textbook. Just like a guided reading lesson with a story from a basal reader, teachers should use a variety of formats to read chapters in social studies or science textbooks. Guiding content-area reading may use a combination of the following:

* <u>Teacher reads aloud</u>. The teacher may want to read aloud the first part of a chapter and any sections that may be particularly difficult to understand.

* <u>Students read aloud</u>. Students who have practiced their parts in advance read from selected parts of the chapter. They provide a model of fluent, efficient reading for their classmates.

* <u>Students read silently</u>. At some point, the children should be asked to read parts of the chapter on their own.

* <u>Rereading</u>. Children having difficulty understanding the textbook can be asked to read the chapter a second time, listen to an audio tape, engage in "buddy reading" with a more able classmate, or read with the teacher in a small-group format. Audio tapes of content-area texts are often available from publishers in both English and Spanish.

Highlight important information. When students are asked to read their social studies or science textbooks, teachers should emphasize essential information in the selection. This should be done while students read and immediately thereafter. There are a number of ways teachers can highlight the important information in a content-area reading assignment:

* <u>Study guides</u>. Middle school and high school teachers have used study guides for years (these are also called "reading guides"). They can also be used effectively with elementary school children. The purpose of all study guides is to focus student attention on key information in the text. Children complete the guides while working in small groups; the guides may be completed by the whole class with the teacher's assistance; or children may asked to complete them individually. Study guides can be constructed in a number of formats.

<u>Key questions</u>. The simplest study guide is a set of questions based on the most important information in the text. With children who have a great deal of difficulty reading content-area material, some teachers even include the page number where the answer can be found. A simple study guide like this would be:

Study Guide – The Russians in California
Pages 122–123

1. Where in Alaska had the Russians built a trading post?
2. Why did Nikolai Rezanov sail to San Francisco?
3. How long did the Russians stay at Fort Ross? Why did they leave?

Pattern study guide. As mentioned previously, a study guide can be based on the structure of the text. This type of study guide typically is an outline with the major topics provided; the students are challenged to fill in the details. For example, below is a study guide, based on the pattern of sequence, for a chapter describing events leading to the Revolutionary War:

Study Guide
Lesson 3: A New British Policy
Pages 247–259

1. 1765: The Stamp Act. Britain placed a tax on colonial _____
2. As a result, some colonists joined the _____
3. 1767: The Townshend Duties: Britain placed a tax on colonial _____
4. As a result, colonial merchants organized a _____
5. 1770: At the Boston Massacre, British soldiers _____
6. 1773: People destroyed tea at the Boston Tea Party because _____
7. 1774: The First Continental Congress voted to _____

Three-level study guide. This type of study guide is sometimes called an interlocking guide and will involve comprehension at three levels: literal, interpretative, and applied. As originally conceived the three-level guide consisted of statements written by the teacher, students then check those that are true. Other three-level guides consist of two or three questions from each of the levels of comprehension.

* Learning logs. Another way teachers can highlight important information is to ask students to keep learning logs while they read content-area material. A learning log is a type of journal students use to record many things: their questions, plans for projects, and ideas for further study. Teachers should use prompts or questions to focus students on essential information. Sometimes the prompts are general (i.e., "List three things you learned today about the Gold Rush in California"), or they may be focused ("Write a letter to your parents explaining why you want to go to California to hunt for gold").

* Data retrieval charts. Data retrieval charts allow students to record information in a framework provided by the teacher. They do not require a great deal of writing and they focus students on the essential information in a selection. Below is a data retrieval chart for a chapter on the United States Congress.

Data Retrieval Chart – The United States Congress

	House of Representatives	Senate
Number of Legislators		
Term of Office		

Minimum age

Presiding officer

Special responsibilities

* <u>ReQuest</u>. This instructional format is best used with a small group of students who are reading a chapter from their social studies or science textbook. The teacher and the students read a part of the chapter silently (a paragraph or a page). The teacher closes his or her book, and the students are invited to ask questions. The teacher answers the questions. Then, the students close their book and the teacher asks questions, usually following up on what the students asked. The students then proceed to the next segment (paragraph or page) and the same procedure is followed. This continues until the teacher feels the students know enough to read the remainder of the chapter with understanding.

Teaching Students to Use Text Structure

In addition to planning and implementing well-designed content-area reading lessons, teachers can also help improve student comprehension of content-area texts by teaching them to use text structures as a tool (again, these expository text structures are cause and effect, problem and solution, comparison/contrast, sequence, and description). This type of instruction is best suited for children in the upper grades. Many lessons must be taught if children are to become efficient at using the text structure to predict, clarify, and summarize. The lessons would take place in a small group format, with a social studies or science textbook. Three things happen in this type of lesson.

(1) Model – The teacher models his or her thought processes as he or she uses the text structure to predict, clarify, or summarize. The teacher explains why he or she recognizes the pattern and focuses on key words.

(2) Recognition – The teacher helps students recognize text structures while they are reading together. The emphasis is on identifying the structure and using it to predict, clarify, or summarize.

(3) Production – As students become proficient in recognizing text structures, teachers ask them to produce a study guide or graphic organizer based on the structure.

Reading for Different Purposes (Skimming, Scanning, In-depth)

Children will have different purposes when reading content-area material, depending on what they hope to accomplish. The process of reading a story or a chapter from a social studies or science textbook is the same – you start at the beginning and read until you come to the end. Many times, however, students need to retrieve only a small piece of information. For example, a teacher asks students to find out the unusual coincidence of the deaths of John Adams and Thomas Jefferson. Students would not want to read the entire encyclopedia entry on either man. Instead they would scan the entry, read quickly, and skip about until they found the dates of each man's death. (The coincidence is that both Adams and Jefferson died on the same day, July 4, 1826, exactly fifty years after the signing of the Declaration of Independence.)

Skimming

Skimming is an extraordinarily fast reading of a text, usually for purposes of preview or review. While skimming, the reader is looking for key words, subtitles, and important sentences. This type of reading develops only with practice. Teachers should model skimming and then challenge students to skim a page or two on their own. Then, the teacher should highlight the key words, phrases, and sentences on those pages.

Scanning

Scanning, on the other hand, is a rapid reading to find specific information. The reader must swiftly sweep over the page, looking for a path to the correct details. As with skimming, this type of reading is learned with practice. The teacher should model scanning and then provide guided practice for children.

In-depth Reading

Finally, some assignments require students to read a content-area selection very carefully, aiming for a full understanding of the information presented. There are many tools students could use to assist themselves in this type of reading. They could develop their own outline, make their own pattern guide, or record important information and their questions in a learning log.

SQ3R is an old technique to help students become proficient at in-depth reading. (it was first proposed in 1946). SQ3R stands for survey, question, read, recite, review. First students survey the chapter they need to read, looking at the title, subtitles, captions, and anything in bold type. Next, they write two or three questions they think the chapter will answer. Third, the students read the chapter, looking for answers to their questions. Fourth, students test themselves on the material presented in the chapter, stating aloud key points. Finally, students periodically review what they have learned, using their written questions and answers as a guide.

Study Skills

Study skills refer to locating and retrieving information from reference materials like almanacs, atlases, encyclopedias, and now, Internet web sites. There are some things teachers should cover with their students.

Encyclopedias

<u>Lessons on the organization of an encyclopedia</u>. Teachers should help students understand that information is organized by topics, called entries, which are arranged in different volumes, in alphabetical order. For example, a first lesson might involve showing students a full set of encyclopedias. Then, the teacher would present some sample entries (archery, Wisconsin, insects) and ask students to identify the volume where the entry would be located.

<u>Lessons on how to use the index, guide words, and cross-references</u>. Once students understand the organization of an encyclopedia, the teacher should then work with students to teach them how to swiftly find information by using the index, the guide words on each page, and the cross-references within each entry. The essential task here is to give children topics and then help them find the relevant pages as quickly as possible.

<u>How to scan for specific information</u>. Finally, once students have located the relevant page number for an entry, they need to practice scanning to find the information they need.

Alternatives to Note-taking

Most elementary school children find it very difficult to take notes while reading reference material. This is an important skill because it allows the reader to preserve important information he or she has found in an almanac, atlas, encyclopedia, or web site. There are many alternatives to standard note-taking for elementary children:

<u>I-Charts</u>. The use of I-Charts (information charts) will help children retrieve and preserve information from reference sources. The I-Chart is a sheet of paper with the following information on it: the student's name, the topic he or she is researching, a subtopic of that topic, a section titled "what I already know," a place to write new information, a place to write the bibliographic information about the reference source, a space for "other related information," a space for "important words," and a space for new questions. Each time a student consults a reference source, he or she completes an I-Chart.

<u>Data Retrieval Charts</u>. These were described above. The teacher creates the framework for the chart and the students write information in the appropriate places.

Chapter 10
Content Area 10:
Student Independent Reading

Introduction

In Chapter 2, Planning, Organizing, and Managing Reading Instruction, I pointed out that the developers of RICA stress that reading instruction should be "balanced." That is, direct instruction in reading skills and strategies should be complemented with opportunities for children to use what they have learned as they read a variety of good books and have opportunities to write about them. Content Area 10 describes what teachers should know and do to encourage children to read as "frequently, broadly, and thoughtfully as possible."

Independent reading refers to reading that takes place at times other than as a part of a teacher-directed lesson. The material children read independently will usually be fiction, but should also include biographies, information books, magazines, and newspapers. Teachers should guide students to high-quality children's books, and in some cases, assign books for their students to read. Most independent reading, however, should be self-selected and self-paced. Reading is self-selected if the child chooses what she will read, and it is self-paced if the child reads the book with no externally imposed deadline.

It is important that children have opportunities to read independently both at school and at home. In fact, the RICA Content Standards have a separate substandard for **at-home reading**.

The RICA Content Standards state that independent reading plays a critical role in a child's overall development as a literate person. Specifically, the Content Standards mention the following advantages of independent reading:

(1) Familiarity with language patterns
(2) Increases fluency
(3) Increases vocabulary
(4) Broadens knowledge in the content areas
(5) Motivates further reading

How to Assess Student Independent Reading

Effective teachers of reading are able to connect children with books that are just right for them. These will be books that are written at the child's independent reading level, and thus are easy to read; and, at the same time, are written by favorite authors, in a favorite genre, or on a favorite topic. To find the right book for each child, teachers will need to know the child's independent reading level and the child's reading interests. It is not easy to get reluctant readers to read, but your best bet is to remember this formula: Independent reading level + Personal interest = Best chance of success.

Teachers also should collect data on the books children read and on each child's independent classroom reading behavior.

Interest Inventory

Reading interest inventories are surveys on student reading behavior. They should be given orally to younger children; our older students can write their answers on the inventory itself. These inventories include two types of questions: (1) those that try to determine to what extent the child values reading as a recreational activity, and (2) those that try to determine the child's reading preferences. Questions on an interest inventory might include:

If your teacher said you can spend one hour doing any school activity you wanted, what would your choose?

How much time each day do you spend reading books at home?

Who is your favorite author?

Which of the following types of books do you like to read? Check as many as you like:

        Animal stories
        Fairy tales
        Mysteries
        Historical fiction (stories that take place in the past)
        Adventures
        High fantasy (such as the Harry Potter books)

As with any form of survey, teachers should be cautious in interpreting the results of an interest inventory, especially with older students. For one thing, many students have learned that reading is important to teachers, and thus will claim to read a lot more than they really do. The results of an interest inventory should be used in concert with the data you gather from student reading logs and your records of individual conferences.

Individual Conferences

Though they require one-to-one settings, teachers should hold regular, individual conferences with their students. During and immediately after these conferences, teachers should take notes. More recently some teachers have been recording these notes on laptop computers. Each child comes to the conference with her journal, where she has written responses to the books she has read; her reading log, a record of the books she has read; and the book she is currently reading. The teacher uses the conference to discuss what the child has read, to help the child find new books to read, and to work on a skill or strategy the child has not mastered. The child may read to the teacher or the teacher may read to the child. The conferences can be expanded to include analysis and discussion of what the child has been writing.

Even if the conferences are held infrequently, like once every two weeks, they yield important data. The teacher will learn about the student's reading interests and ability. The results of the conferences can be compared to the information gained through the interest inventory and the student's reading log.

Student Reading Logs/Journals

Each student should keep a record of the books he or she has read independently. A child in the first and second grade can write the name of each book, the book's author, the date he finished the book, and a personal response on a 3 x 5 card. The cards can be held together with yarn or stored in a file box. Older children should enter the same information on a reading log, which is kept in a folder. Yes, it is true that some children may commit fraud and enter books they haven't finished in order to impress the teacher. The results of individual conferences and common sense, however, will allow you to determine who has been "fudging." These reading logs will give you important information on the independent reading habits of your students.

In Chapter 8 on Literary Response and Analysis, I wrote that teachers should require students to write journal responses to the books they have read. While the substance of those responses primarily is useful to determine their development in the areas of response and analysis, the responses can also be used to make judgments about their level of independent reading. Simply put, children who read a lot independently will have full responses to more books than children who do not.

Data on Reading Behavior at School and at Home

It is a good idea to write anecdotal notes about the reading behavior of your students at school. For example, at lunch on a rainy day, who decides to read? During your visits to the school library, who thoughtfully selects a book and begins reading and who, on the other hand, seems to waste time and avoid reading?

Gathering data about reading behavior at home is more difficult. Some teachers send surveys home asking parents about their child's reading behavior. Such surveys have questionable validity because some parents will not know how much their children read and others may report a level of reading that is inaccurate. Other teachers, especially those in the upper grades, ask students to keep a log of their at-home reading for a period of a couple of weeks.

Independent Reading Level

Teachers should know the independent reading levels of all their students by administering an IRI. This information is essential in helping children read more. A teacher who knows the reading interests and the reading levels of his or her students will have the necessary information to connect children to books they will want to read.

What Teachers Can Do to Promote Independent and At-Home Reading

Encouraging Independent Reading in School

Daily Opportunities for Self-Selected Reading

Sustained Silent Reading (SSR). SSR is a time when everyone in the classroom reads silently. This should be the same time every day, and may be as little as five minutes a day during the first weeks of first grade to 30 minutes a day in a sixth grade classroom. Children select their own reading material, which may be books, newspapers, encyclopedias, magazines, or their textbooks. It is very important that everybody, the teacher and any visitors to the room included, read silently. No interruptions are acceptable. SSR also is sometimes called DEAR (Drop Everything and Read).

Readers/writers workshop. During the height of the Whole Language movement, many teachers used an instructional program format called readers workshop. This was a hour or more a day when children read silently, small groups worked on projects, and the teacher met with individual students and groups of children who shared a similar need. The format was often expanded to include both reading and writing.

The balanced, comprehensive approach advocated by the developers of RICA, however, makes it impractical for teachers to use readers/writers workshop every day. It simply isn't a format conducive to the amount of direct, explicit teaching required by a program following the RICA guidelines. Recently, I have seen teachers with balanced reading programs who use readers/writers workshop one or two days a week. This provides time for direct instruction and time for students to do a great deal of reading and writing.

Frequent Opportunities to Share What Has Been Read

Children should have many opportunities to talk and write about the books they have read. The experience of sharing reading experiences can motivate children to read more independently.

Reading journals. As mentioned previously, children should be required to write responses to books they have read independently in their journals. Teachers can provide generic prompts ("Let's write about the setting of the books we are reading independently") or simply say "Please take out your journal and write something about the book you are reading." The key is that the journals should become interactive – the teacher should write back to the student.

Individual conferences. There is nothing more valuable than the opportunity to talk to your students in a one-to-one setting. While many things can be accomplished in an individual conference, such as individual skill and strategy instruction, it is important that the teacher and the student have a conversation about the books the student has read.

Literature circles, response groups, grand conversations, book clubs.
All of these names refer to the same type of discussion format – a small group of students who are reading the same book, just like the book clubs some adults belong to. They meet occasionally while they read the book and immediately after they have finished. For example, in a fifth grade classroom, one group is reading Holes by Louis Sachar, another Ella Enchanted by Gail Carson Levine and the third, Bud, Not Buddy by Christopher Paul Curtis. The teacher's role is to ask questions and to say as little as possible. The questions should be open-ended and provocative in that they have a good chance to spark spirited discussions. Some teachers use a more structured format, assigning roles to students (one is the "moderator", another is the "recorder," etc.) and using a generic set of questions all groups must answer.

Promoting Books

In addition to assessing independent student reading and encouraging children to read, teachers must also guide children to high-quality children's books from a wide range of genres written by diverse authors.

Reading Aloud

Almost all elementary school teachers read aloud daily to their students. This is a good way to introduce students to the best of children's literature. Teachers who read aloud effectively, with enthusiasm and dramatic effect, can impact the reading habits of their students. The key is to bring books that are "related" to the read aloud selection to class. For example, if a teacher is reading aloud The Runaway Bunny to a class of first graders, he or she should bring to class other books written by Margaret Wise Brown, like Goodnight, Moon, or books such as The Little Island by Golden MacDonald. A sixth grade teacher who reads aloud The Book of Three, the first book in Lloyd Alexander's five-book series, "The Chronicles of Prydain," should have copies of the second book in the series, The Black Cauldron.

Booktalks

Booktalks are "sales pitches," where the teacher tries to "sell" students on a book. The teacher displays the book, talks about the characters and setting (without giving away the story, of course), and reads an excerpt. Then, hopefully, some children will want to read the book.

Books Connected to Other Areas of the Curriculum

Teachers should have in the classroom a collection of books (20 – 30) that are connected to units of study in social studies, science, and the arts. This is good time to encourage children to read information books. For example, a fifth grade classroom studying Colonial America should have copies of information books like Edwin Tunis' Colonial Living and fiction like The Witch of Blackbird Pond by Elizabeth George Speare.

Trips to the Library

Even in this Information Age, it is important that children become familiar with how to use the library. Every classroom should have a library of books. There should be books at the reading level of every child in the room. All classrooms should regularly visit the school library so children can learn how library books are organized and how to check out books. Each class should annually take a trip to the local public library. Some fortunate schools are within walking distance of public libraries, and monthly "walking" field trips are a possibility. To promote books and independent reading, all children should have public library cards.

Supporting At-Home Reading

Encourage Kids to Read at Home

A number of variables, of course, make it difficult for teachers to change at-home reading behavior. To encourage children to read at home, teachers can do the following:

Let children take books from the classroom or school library home. Both your classroom and school libraries should have check-out systems so that everyone knows which books a child has borrowed. The vast majority of children will return books promptly. Some children will struggle with returning books, and in those cases, teachers and parents must work together to help children be responsible.

Get children excited about books. I have seen classrooms where a teacher reads aloud the first chapter of book to a literature study group and the children are so excited they can't wait to get home so they can finish the book. You might review all the ideas I shared previously about how to encourage independent reading and promote books. Hopefully, your enthusiasm will "spill over" and stimulate at-home reading.

SSR at home. Some teachers have had success in working with parents so that every child has a period of sustained, silent reading at home. This requires communication with parents and their support for this practice.

Support Parents

Virtually all parents want their children to become good readers and are willing to work with teachers to support the at-home reading of their children. Here are some ideas to support parents:

Encourage SSR at home. This requires a high level of parental and sibling support. If SSR time is from 7:30 to 8:00 on Mondays and Thursdays, this means everybody in the house reads, and this means the phone isn't answered and the television is turned off.

Provide lists of books that can be checked out of the public library. Parents of kindergarteners and first graders welcome a list of books that they can read aloud to their children. Teachers can also prepare lists of books for children to read on their own. I know one teacher who provided each parent with a list of "Fifty Great Books for Fourth Graders." Lists of information books on topics in social studies and science also should be sent home.

Provide information on local public library. Teachers can encourage parents to take their children to the public library. A packet should be sent home with maps, times of operation, and information on how to acquire a library card.

Use the first languages of your English Language Learners. Almost 40% of our K-12 school population has acquired English as a second language. We can support our English Language Learners (ELLs) by acknowledging their bilingual status. All communication with parents should be in the language the parent understands. Parents should be encouraged to read to their children in their native language and, if possible, in English. During SSR at home, it doesn't make any difference which language people read in since our goal is the development of the "reading habit." Lists of good books written in a language other than English at public libraries should be made available to parents.

Support family literacy projects. Many elementary schools have established programs to improve the literacy of parents in the community. While these programs require the expertise of a specialist, classroom teachers can support family literacy projects by disseminating information and supporting parents who participate.

Chapter 11
Content Area 11:
Supporting Reading Through Oral and
Written Language Development

Introduction

It is important to note the title of this content area – <u>supporting</u> reading through oral and written language development. The RICA Content Specifications indicate that the focus of this area is the <u>interrelationships</u> among reading, writing, speaking, and listening. Teachers should understand the linkages among the four language arts and see how instruction in oral and writing development can enhance reading proficiency.

How to Assess Oral and Written Language

The RICA Content Specifications state that teachers should be "able to informally assess students' oral and written language and use that information when planning reading instruction."

For both oral and written language, <u>audience</u> and <u>purpose</u> should determine the substance and form of what a person says and writes. For example, a shopping list for Saturday's visit to the supermarket will include only sparse descriptions of the items to be purchased and it may be rather sloppy. The purpose is very limited and the audience is one – the person doing the shopping. On the other hand, an essay written as part of a job application will look quite different. The writer likely will prepare some sort of outline, compose a rough draft, edit, and revise. The final draft will be polished and should address the issues the employer considers significant. Thus, the simplest assessment of oral and written language is: <u>Does the comment or written product achieve the speaker's (or writer's) purpose by reaching the speaker's (or writer's) audience?</u>

There are two aspects of oral and written language which teachers can assess: (1) substance and (2) form. Assessments of substance focus on <u>what</u> the student said or wrote, while assessments of form focus on <u>how</u> the student said it or wrote it.

For example, for oral language, teachers should gather data to determine whether or not children "stay on topic." When asked a question, do they provide an answer that is direct and to the point? When they take part in a discussion, do they respond to what others have said or do they bring up extraneous points? When making an oral presentation, have they provided relevant information? These questions get to the substance of their oral comments. For writing, the teacher would ask similar questions.

Assessments of the <u>form</u> of their oral production focus on choice of words and organization. Are children clear and coherent when they speak? When answering a question, do students emphasize the most relevant points? In discussions and in oral presentations, are their comments organized appropriately? In writing, assessment of form focuses on organization and writing mechanics (spelling, punctuation, usage).

For both oral and written language development, teachers can use one of three formats to assess student development:

Qualitative assessment. Qualitative assessments are written summaries of student performance. The teacher's written comments may focus on any aspect of what the student has said or written. When kept over a long period of time, these anecdotal records are important pieces of data.

Holistic quantitative assessment. Quantitative assessment uses numbers to describe student performance. Holistic assessment uses a single criterion. For example, if a teacher is assessing students taking part in a literature discussion, the teacher may be judging students on how well they incorporate the comments of others in their own comments. Student would be ranked; for example, from 1 to 3. A "1" would be assigned to students who never mention the comments of others, a "2" would be given to students who occasionally mention the comments of others, and a "3" would be given to students who frequently mention the comments of others.

Analytic quantitative assessment. Analytic assessment uses multiple criteria and then sums those scores for a total. For example, on a written assignment students might be graded from 1 to 5 on (a) capitalization, (b) spelling, (c) topic sentences, and (d) a conclusion.

Rubrics. Teachers will need rubrics to assess student writing if they are using some form of quantitative analysis. The rubrics state criteria and provide descriptors for numerical scores. Please note:

*The rubric can be holistic, based on a single criteria; or analytic, based on multiple criteria.

* The rubric can focus solely on substance. For example, students writing an essay on the theme of forgiveness in the novel *Out of the Dust* by Karen Hesse might have this substance-focused rubric:

> 1. Fails to mention how either Billie Jo or her father forgive each other; fails to mention issue of self-forgiveness; fails to mention any specific episodes in the book
>
> 2. Focuses on one character (Billie Jo or her father) but fails to mention the role played by the other character; at least one specific episode discussed
>
> 3. Discusses both Billie Jo and her father, and the importance of self-forgiveness, and cites relevant episodes in the book

* The rubric can focus solely on form. For example, a paper could be assessed just on the criteria of spelling.

The rubric can be mixed and categorize papers on criteria based on both form and substance. For example, to get a 5, the highest mark possible, a paper would have to match the following criteria: Paper has no errors in spelling or punctuation, takes a position on an issue, and has supporting details.

Assessing Oral Language During Reading-Related Activities

Again, teachers should assess oral language development by using (a) anecdotal, qualitative recordkeeping, (b) holistic, quantitative scoring, and (c) analytic, quantitative scoring. The following reading-related activities can be used to assess oral language development:

Small Group Literature Discussions

Small group discussions about books provide an ideal opportunity for teachers to gather data on oral language development. Sometimes teachers should take anecdotal notes. This is an effective way to make a record of the "bumps on the horizon" – the events that stand out. For example, a teacher might write the names of students who say nothing. Another time, the teacher might make a record of the comments of a student who was particularly insightful.

Teachers should also use quantitative methods to assess student performance during literature discussion. A teacher could use the following criteria for any discussion: (a) listens attentively to others, (b) takes turns, does not interrupt, (c) asks questions to clarify, (d) expands on what others say, and (e) makes comments relevant to the topic. Criteria related to literature could be linked to the literary elements. For example, if the focus of the assessment is on character, the teacher might use the following criteria: comments show the student understands the character's motivation for acting the way she or he did in the story.

Language Play

Children in the primary grades will take part in "language play" to develop phonemic awareness and learn the sound-symbol relationships of the English language. Students will chant rhymes, poems, and songs. Teachers should gather data on their oral language development when they do so.

Drama Based On Literature

Children in all grades should take part in dramatic performances based on children's books. The two most frequently used formats are reader's theater (when children read their lines) and plays. Drama activities provide teachers with opportunities to gather data on the ability of children to (a) learn their parts and (b) change the way they talk to fit the traits of the characters they are portraying.

Answers to Questions

During many comprehension-building activities, like a guided reading lesson, teachers ask students questions about what they have read. The teacher's primary focus, of course, is on the substance of the student's answer. Teachers also can use this opportunity to assess the oral language development of their students, especially their ability to summarize information coherently.

Assessing Written Language Development During Reading-Related Activities

Once again, teachers will need to gather data on the substance and form of student writing. As for substance, teachers will ask questions about the content of student-authored essays, stories, and poetry. At the same time, teachers will be concerned about the form of what students have written – particularly the organization and mechanics of written products (spelling, punctuation, capitalization).

As with oral language, teachers will gather qualitative data through anecdotal records and develop rubrics for holistic and analytic scoring. Teachers should keep **portfolios** of student writing. The contents of a portfolio will allow teachers to see the longitudinal growth of their students. A portfolio is a place of storage, and may be as simple as a manila folder. Along with pieces of writing the teacher wants to save, most teachers will allow students to select their own favorite pieces for inclusion in the portfolio.

All of the following reading-related activities can be used to make evaluations about student writing development:

* Journals with responses to literature

* Stories based on the characters, setting, theme, or style of a book

* Answers to questions written as part of reading lessons

* Essays about issues and themes raised in books

* Captions to illustrations from books

How to Teach:
Oral Language Development and Reading

Reading-related oral language activities challenge students to talk in ways that meet their purpose and reach their audience. Here are some reading-related oral language activities that teachers should implement with their students:

Language Play to Develop Phonics and Phonemic Awareness

Language play includes chants, rhymes, poems, songs, anything that focuses on the sounds of words. These activities will develop phonemic awareness and can help children understand the sound-symbol relationships of English. Most of these oral activities are done in choral fashion (more than one child talks at a time).

Drama

Good literature should serve as the basis for dramatic projects in the elementary classroom. Entire books, parts of books, and abridgements of books can be used as the script for plays and reader's theater presentations (remember, in reader's theater, the child-actors read their parts). Dramatic projects demand a different kind of oral proficiency than that required by conversation or classroom recitation. The child must adapt the way she speaks to fit the character she is portraying.

Group Discussions of Books

Small group discussions provide children with excellent opportunities to develop their oral proficiency. Children will learn how to speak clearly and concisely, how to be a good listener, how to take turns, and how to respond to the comments of others. Children's literature provides the topics for these conversations.

The groups should be small, from three to six members. The teacher plays several roles. At first, he or she should model good group conversation skills (i.e., by disagreeing without being disagreeable – "That's a good point, Fred, and I agree with most of what you said, but I think . . ."). Ultimately, the teacher becomes a facilitator, saying as little as possible to keep the conversation going.

Children should learn the rules of productive group discussions: (1) don't interrupt, (2) don't dominate, (3) address ideas – not people, (4) clarify other's comments, (5) expand on other's comments, and (6) state your perspectives clearly and support them with details.

Answering Questions

During and after children read, typically as part of a guided reading lesson, teachers will ask them to answer questions. This is an excellent way to help children develop the ability to "think on their feet." Answers to higher level comprehension questions (inference, cause-effect relationships, generalizing, and evaluating) will challenge students to think critically before they express themselves.

Sharing Content Information after Content-Area Reading

Students will read content-area texts to gather information (once again, content-area material includes social studies textbooks, science textbooks, encyclopedias, and Internet sites). Though the traditional oral report can be a boring experience for all, many teachers help children develop their formal oral presentation skills by teaching their students how to organize what they are going to say and use visual aids to support the message.

How to Teach:
Written Language Development and Reading

The Writing Process

Many reading-related activities will allow children to become more proficient in each phase of the writing process. For example, after students have read E. B. White's Stuart Little, they may write a sequel describing Stuart's further adventures. While some writing tasks do not require the use of each stage of the writing process, like writing a grocery list, most writing tasks do. Here is a quick summary of the writing process.

Stage one: Prewriting. Here, students choose or narrow their topic. They should learn how to consider their purpose and audience before deciding on the form of the final written product. Children will generate main ideas and organize supporting detail. This can be accomplished by making a semantic web (cluster), talking to classmates, doing a "quick write," drawing a pictures, or writing an outline.

Stage two: Drafting. Using the prewriting product as a basis, the student composes a first draft.

Stage three: Revising/editing. During this phase someone needs to edit the first draft. The editor can be the writer herself, a teacher, or classmates. The writer then makes revisions based on the editor's suggestions.

Stage four: Final draft. Usually the revision completed in stage three will be the final draft. For some pieces of writing, however, multiple copies of a final draft will be made for multiple readers.

Journals

As part of experiences with literature and with content-area texts, elementary school children will write in journals. Journal writing is informal. The journals themselves can be composition books or simply paper in a folder. Experiences with high-quality children's books, especially, can be used as a basis for each of the following types of journals:

Personal journals. Personal journals are private and should be read only by the student and the teacher.

Dialogue journals. In this type of journal, the entries are meant to be shared. A classmate or the teacher reads the entries in the journal and then writes a response.

Reading logs/Reader response journals. In this category of journal, students record the date they begin and the date they finish reading a book. As they read the book, intermediate level and older students write journal entries, noting how characters or events make them feel. All students complete their journal entries by writing about the book after they finish reading it.

Double entry journals. Students divide each journal page in half. One kind of information is written on one side and another type of information is written on the other half. An example is "quotes and notes," a type of double-entry journal in which the student writes a direct quote from a book and then a response.

Content learning logs. This type of journal is used in social studies and science. Students write down questions they want answered, copy assignments, and list important information they have learned.

Writing Stories

Experiences with children's books can serve as the basis for creative writing experiences. Once they have learned about story grammars, story frames, and story maps, children can use these devices during the prewriting phase of the writing process. Our youngest children may need to start by first creating the illustrations and then writing the text to their stories.

Our Youngest Writers

Our youngest writers, kindergarteners and first graders, will complete a variety of written assignments, each with the goal of helping children master the intricacies of writing in English.

* How to write each letter of the alphabet. When teachers teach students to recognize the 26 letters of the English alphabet, they should, at the same time, teach them to write the letters.

* Interactive Writing. Children's literature can serve as the basis for many interactive writing experiences. Interactive writing is an instructional format in which children and their teacher create a text together – actually sharing the pen as the text is

written on a piece of chart paper or an overhead projector. The teacher and the children compose together.

      * Language Experience Approach. This is a good activity for showing children that their ideas can be preserved through writing (see Chapter 4 for a description).

      * Captions for illustrations. This is an excellent beginning writing activity. Young children draw a picture, and first dictate a caption. Then, at some point, they write the caption themselves.

Literature and Modes (or Genres) of Writing

Through their experiences with literature, older students can learn to write in many different modes (these different types of writing are also called written "genres"). These modes include forms of poetry, ABC books, fairy tales, myths, mysteries, and science fiction.

Expository Modes

Finally, children need to become proficient in writing expository (informational) text. Experiences with content-area material will help children see the difference between expository and narrative (stories) texts. Some of the expository modes that children should be taught to write include brief descriptions of persons, places, or events; friendly letters; formal letters; summaries with main ideas and supporting details; persuasive letters; and reports based on information gathered from several sources. Expository writing might require students to use expository text patterns and include writing about cause-and-effect relationships; writing about a problem and its solution; comparing or contrasting concepts, ideas, or events; sequencing events; and writing content descriptions and supporting these descriptions with details and examples.

How to Teach:
English Language Learners and Reading

English Language Learners (ELLs) are children who are acquiring English as a second language. Previously, these children were described as students of Limited English Proficiency (LEPs). The ELL descriptor is now more widely used. As you have probably learned in your teacher preparation classes, over one-third of California's K-12 students are ELLs. The RICA Content Specifications expect beginning teachers to be able to:

      * Interrelate the elements of language arts instruction to support the reading development of English language learners (e.g., using preview-review, visual aids, charts, real objects, word organizers, graphic organizers, and outlining).

* Know general ways in which the writing systems of other languages may differ from English (e.g., that not all writing systems are alphabetic, that English is less regular phonetically than some other alphabetic languages).

* Understand factors and processes involved in transferring literacy competencies from one language to another (e.g., positive and negative transfer) and use knowledge of language similarities and differences to promote transfer of language skills (e.g., through scaffolding strategies, modeling, and explicit instruction).

Instruction to Support the Reading Development of English Language Learners

The key concept here is that teachers need to provide **scaffolding** for reading lessons with ELLs. A scaffold is some instructional intervention that assists the student in learning. This is the same concept as **sheltered** instruction – the teacher builds the learning scaffold so that the ELL achieves the same objectives as everybody else. In California, this type of instruction is called specially designed academic instruction in English **(SDAIE).** Teachers can support the reading development of their ELLs by selecting any or all of the following interventions:

Preview-review. A preview of the lesson, including the objective, is given in the student's first language (i.e., Vietnamese, Spanish, etc.). After the lesson, a review of what was learned is provided in the first language. Obviously, this requires a teacher, aide, or student who is bilingual.

Visual aids/Real objects. Reading lessons, especially vocabulary lessons, should be supported by photographs and illustrations. With ELLs, a picture is worth a thousand words. Even better than a photograph or illustration, however, would be to use real objects to teach essential vocabulary before children read (i.e., to teach the meaning of *asparagus*, the best thing a teacher can do is to allow students to handle real asparagus while the teacher gives the students the words to identify and describe it).

Charts. Before, during, or after ELLs are asked to read a content-area text, a chart summarizing essential information will help the children read with greater understanding. Illustrations and charts may further facilitate understanding.

Graphic organizers/Outlines. Graphic organizers (see Chapter 9) or a simple outline displayed before ELLs read will help them activate their background knowledge and predict what they are about to read.

Teacher model/Explicit instruction. Two instructional practices will help ELLs during reading lessons. First, it is important that teachers model any behavior they want students to do. If, for example, a word is to be circled in a workbook page, then the teacher should make a plastic transparency of the page and demonstrate on the overhead projector the drawing of a circle around the correct answer. Second, teachers should be absolutely clear when they ask ELLs to do something. Lessons with a single objective and simple-to-follow instructions will increase the chances ELLs will be successful.

English and Other Writing Systems

English is an **alphabetic** system. In an alphabetic system, letters represent sounds. Some other languages are alphabetic but do not use the same 26 letters as English. My word processor produced the following phrases, for example:

In Greece, people use the Greek alphabet:

Γρεεκ υσεσ τηε Γρεεκ αλπηαβετ

In the Ukraine, people use the Cyrillic alphabet:

Υκρανιαν υσεσ τηε Χψριλλιχ αλπηαβετ

Chinese, on the other hand, is a **logographic** system. Symbols represent words (actually, in linguistic terms, the symbols represent morphemes). In a logographic system there are thousands of symbols.

Transfer from One Language to Another

Once children learn to read in one language, there is much they can transfer to learning a second language.

Concepts about print. ELLs who have learned to read in their first language will have acquired several concepts about print. They will have the general idea that print carries meaning. They will know the parts of books. They may also have acquired the sense of directionality of printed texts (assuming that their first language moves left to right, top to bottom, like English).

Vocabulary. If the ELL's first language belongs to the Romance family (French, Italian, Portuguese, Romanian, or Spanish) or is a member of the Germanic family of languages (German, Dutch, Swedish, etc.), then there is a good chance that some English vocabulary has already been learned because the English word is similar to the same word in the student's first language. (i.e., the English word *field* is almost identical to the German *feld* and the Dutch *veld*).

Reading habits and behaviors. Children who have learned to read in their first language will have acquired certain habits and behaviors that will help them become literate in English. For example, they will know that some texts must be read silently, and that requires a quiet time and a quite place. ELLs who can read well in their first language probably know about libraries – how to check books out, how to behave in a library.

Chapter 12:
Content Area 12:
Vocabulary Development

Introduction

A *vocabulary* is a set of words. It is important to note that each person has five different vocabularies.

Listening vocabulary. These are the words that a person understands when listening to other people speak.

Speaking vocabulary. Your speaking vocabulary is the words you use when you talk, and this vocabulary is always smaller than your listening vocabulary.

Writing vocabulary. This vocabulary consists of the words you use when you write.

Sight (reading) vocabulary. A child's sight vocabulary consists of the words he or she can recognize and correctly pronounce. We discussed this in Chapter 5.

Meaning (reading) vocabulary. A child's meaning vocabulary consists of the words he or she can understand when reading silently. The focus of this chapter is on meaning – helping children expand their knowledge of word meanings.

Research shows that there are three things that teachers should do to expand the meaning vocabularies of their students:

(1) Increase the amount of time children read independently and increase the different types of books they read,

(2) Teach children the meanings of important words, and

(3) Teach children strategies they can implement independently to figure out the meanings of words they do not know.

How to Assess Vocabulary Development

Assessing Word Meaning

For meaning vocabulary, teachers can select standardized, commercially published tests, like the Comprehensive Tests of Basic Skills (CTBS) and the Stanford Achievement Tests (SAT); vocabulary tests that come with a basal reader series; or tests they have designed themselves to assess a student's level of word meaning. Here are some formats for assessing meaning vocabulary:

Word in sentence/Multiple answer options. Standardized tests and the tests that come with a basal reader series usually adopt this format for testing meaning vocabulary. A target word, underlined or italicized, appears in a phrase or a sentence. The test-taker then must select a correct definition from four options.

Choose a synonym. Another way to test knowledge of word meanings is to ask students to identify a synonym to a target word.

Analogies. A third format that can be used to assess meaning vocabulary is the use of analogies. Two words are listed together, there is a relationship between the two, and then the target word appears. The student must select a word that has that same relationship to the target word. For example, *head* is to *body* as _____ is to *mountain* (the correct answer is *peak*).

Match definition to word. Finally, another possible way to assess word meaning is to provide children with a list of words and a list of possible definitions. Then, they must match the proper definition with each word.

Tests of Morphemic Analysis

Tests of morphemic analysis assess student knowledge of prefixes, suffixes, root words, and compound words. These are also sometimes called tests of "structural analysis." Some tests ask students to identify nonsense words with common prefixes or suffixes (i.e., *monotell, semidid*), but these are really tests of prefix and suffix identification, rather than meaning. Other, more meaning-oriented tests ask students to define common prefixes and suffixes (i.e., *What is the difference between a test and a pretest?*).

How to Teach Vocabulary

Read More and Read More Types of Books

Research shows that children learn the meanings of thousands of words simply through independent reading. Many proficient readers have acquired large vocabularies by reading extensively. A phenomenon one authority called the "Matthew Effect" definitely takes place – more able readers tend to read more, and when they do, the gap between them and their less able classmates widens (the descriptor comes from the Bible passage in Matthew about the rich getting richer). Students who need to become better readers must enhance their meaning vocabularies. One way to achieve this goal is to help the child spend more time reading. Another is to expand the types of books the child reads. The more a child reads, the more words she or he will encounter in print. Though researchers cannot explain exactly why, the more often a reader comes across a word, the better chance the reader will acquire an understanding of the word's meaning. Reading books by different authors or in different genres exposes the reader to new types of words.

We discussed how to increase student independent reading in Chapter 10.

Methods of Teaching the Meaning of Words

There are dozens of effective techniques for teaching children the meaning of words. First, a couple of important points. Most teachers try to teach the meaning of too many words each week. Researchers at the University of Pittsburgh have shown there is a magic number – the "average" elementary school student can learn the meanings of about 350–400 words a year. That comes out to about nine a week. Thus, teachers should carefully select the words they teach each week. The words selected should be words that students don't know, words that they are capable of learning, and words that are important in that their meaning is essential if children are to understand the stories or textbook chapters they will be asked to read.

Though many alternatives exist, most teachers rely on two relatively ineffective techniques to teach the meanings of words. The teacher simply displays the word on the blackboard and then tells the children what it means. Likewise, asking children to look up the meaning of a word in a dictionary, without some discussion of the results, is also an ineffective way to teach meaning vocabulary. Here are some worthwhile alternatives:

Cluing Technique

Joan Gipe created the cluing technique as a way to teach the meaning of new words. The teacher creates four sentences for each word that will be taught. The first sentence uses the target word appropriately in a sentence. The second sentence describes the characteristics of the target word. The third sentence defines the target word in language the children will understand. The fourth sentence asks a question with the target word.

The students read the sentences, or the teacher reads the sentences to them. Then the students write an answer to the question in the fourth sentence. Afterwards, the teacher and the students discuss their responses, focusing on the definition of the word. Here is an example for the word *unicycle:*

Fred's older brother rides around on a unicycle. This looks strange because a unicycle has only one wheel. A unicycle is like a bicycle, except it has only one wheel. Would you like to learn how to ride a unicycle?

Contextual Redefinition

Contextual redefinition makes use of the context surrounding the target word and the power of co-operative learning. It is especially effective when teaching words from a story in a basal reader or from a chapter in a social studies or science textbook. First, the teacher finds the paragraph where the target word first appears in the basal reader (or textbook). For simple words, the teacher needs only to copy the sentence in which the target word first appears. For more difficult words, the teacher should copy the sentence preceding that sentence and the sentence superceding it (three sentences in all). The sentences can be placed on a worksheet or on the overhead projector. For example:

There was no system of government like we know it in the mining camps. The miners became <u>vigilantes</u> and caught and punished people who they thought had committed crimes. People were sometimes caught by the vigilantes, given a quick trial, and hung all in the same day.

Contextual redefinition works best with a small group of children. The lesson proceeds as follows:

First, the teacher displays the word and students guess what it means. Those who venture a guess should explain the rationale for their definition. Working as a group, the students come up with one "best-guess" definition. Then the students (or the teacher) read the three sentences. Now, the students guess again what the word means, using the sentences as a basis. Again, they group needs to reach a consensus. If at this point the students have not arrived at a reasonable definition, the teacher should display a dictionary definition.

Semantic Mapping (also called a Word Map or Semantic Webbing)

Semantic maps are diagrams. They are particularly useful in pre-reading instruction because they not only teach the meanings of words, they also help children activate their prior knowledge of key concepts associated with the target word.

The teacher places the target word in the center of a circle. The circle can be written on the blackboard or on a piece of chart paper. The goal is to draw a web of words and phrases around the centered target word. The teacher may supply some words on the chart, but most should come from the students. As new words are suggested, their association to the target word is discussed. Closely-related words should be circled and lines between groups of words should be drawn (these lines look like "rays" coming from the centered circle with the target word).

For example, for the target word *dolphin*, one "satellite" group of words would relate to mammals (breathes, doesn't lay eggs), another to the physical characteristics of dolphins (looks like a big fish, smiles at you), and a third to other associations (smart, talk to each other, named Flipper).

Word Sort (also called List-Group-Label)

In this vocabulary teaching activity, students sort a collection of words. A word sort only works if the target words can be placed in three, four, or five groups. The words should be placed on 3x5 inch cards. The teacher and the students discuss each word and then create categories. For example, for words from a story in a basal reader, the categories might be *characters, setting, events*. These categories are written on the board, and the students place each word in the correct category. This activity works well as a review of words previously learned.

Semantic Feature Analysis

Semantic feature analysis is a strong vocabulary teaching activity for a set of words that share at least one characteristic. It works well with words from social studies and science units. The teacher creates a grid or matrix that identifies traits of the target words. Along the vertical axis, the target words are listed. Along the horizontal axis, the traits are listed. Next to each word, the children place a + under each trait the word shares. If I were to create a grid to help you understand the meaning of vocabulary that identifies strategies for teaching word meaning, you might complete the grid in the following way:

	Teaches meaning vocabulary	Uses context	Uses a chart
Cluing Technique	+	+	-
Contextual Redefinition	+	+	-
Semantic Map	+	-	+
Word Sort	+	-	+
Semantic Feature Analysis	+	-	+

Teaching Word Learning Strategies

In addition to teaching the meanings of words, teachers should also provide children with tools to figure out the meaning of unknown words when they read independently. Two strategies are particularly useful: the use of context and morphemic analysis.

Context Clues

Many times, readers will be able to correctly guess the meaning of an unknown word by thinking about the words, phrases, and sentences that surround that word. Thus, the context of the reading passage will provide clues to the meaning of an unknown word.

Many times, readers will be able to correctly guess the meaning of an unknown word by thinking about the words, phrases, and sentences that surround that word. Thus, the context of the reading passage will provide clues to the meaning of an unknown word.

As I mentioned earlier, there are two types of clues: <u>semantic clues</u> (the meanings of surrounding words) and <u>syntactic clues</u> (clues based on word order, what part of speech the word must be). Here is how teachers can help their students become more proficient at using context clues.

General Approach to Teaching Children to Use Context Clues

The teacher prepares a set of paragraphs, each paragraph contains a word that the children don't know. The teacher then models the following process, using an overhead projector:

First, read aloud the entire paragraph, stopping at the target word for a moment and commenting, "Mmmm . . . I don't think I know what that word is." Continue reading aloud the remainder of the paragraph. Second, go back and underline the unknown word, saying it aloud one more time. Third, reread the paragraph aloud, saying, "I am now going to reread the paragraph and see what words might help me figure out the word I don't know. I will circle any word or group of words that might help me figure out the unknown word." Fourth, after circling the "helper" words, say "I think the unknown word names something and means _____." Finally, take a guess at the unknown word and check the definition provided in a dictionary.

Next, you want students to perform each step independently. You might start by highlighting the unknown word and helping children identify the "helper" words in the paragraph. Eventually, you want students to use context clues without underlining and circling words.

Opin

An Opin sentence is a form of CLOZE, with only one word missing. For example:

During recess, Fred tripped on the _____ and skinned his knee (elephant, rug, asphalt).

One of the word options should clearly be wrong (in this case, *elephant*). A second choice should be close to being correct (*rug*). One of the three choices, of course, should be correct (*asphalt*). Students work in groups of three to decide which word to place in the blank. First, each child makes a selection, then the group talks about their choices. The teacher works with children so that they use the other words in the sentence as clues for determining the correct choice.

Morphemic Analysis

Morphemic analysis requires students to look at the parts of words to determine their meaning. This is also called <u>structural analysis</u>. First, you should know some linguistic words and phrases relating to the structure of words.

Definitions

A <u>morpheme</u> is the most elemental unit of meaning in a language. In English, there are only two types of morphemes, words with and without affixes (prefixes and suffixes). Remember, not all syllables are morphemes, and some words have more than one morpheme.

<u>Affixes</u> are <u>prefixes</u>, morphemes that appear before a root word; and <u>suffixes</u>, morphemes that appear at the end of a root word. Examples of prefixes are *non–*, *un–*, and *pre–*. Examples of suffixes are *–ment, –er,* and *–ly.* (In some languages, but not in English, there is a third type of affix; an infix, which is a morpheme that appears in the middle of a word!)

<u>Bound morphemes</u> are prefixes and suffixes that cannot occur alone, they must be attached to root word (*un–, –est).* A <u>free morpheme</u> is one that can be uttered alone with meaning (for example, *test*).

Teachers should teach their students the following to help them unlock the definitions of unknown words: prefixes, suffixes, common root words, synonyms and antonyms, and Greek and Latin roots and affixes (such as *graph, morph, form*).

A Format for Teaching Prefixes, Suffixes, and Root Words

As with phonics, you can either follow a whole-to-part or part-to-whole approach to teach students about root words and the use of prefixes and suffixes. In a whole-to-part lesson you would follow these steps:

(1) Display several sentences, each with a word that contains the target prefix, suffix, or root word. For example, for the prefix *un–:*

Roberto was <u>unafraid</u> when he entered the haunted house.
The zookeeper <u>uncaged</u> the tiger when it was time to move him to another zoo.
Thuy checked very carefully, but the letter was <u>undated</u>.
The movie was so long it seemed to be <u>unending</u>.
Laticia tried her best but she could not <u>untangle</u> the cord to the Christmas lights.

(2) Read again the underlined target words, and identify the key common element. You might want to circle the common prefix, suffix, or root word.

(3) Work with the students to arrive at the meaning of the prefix, suffix, or root word. If they can't figure it out, tell them what it means.

(4) Provide some other words with the common element, or see if the children can provide the words.

(5) You may want to create a word wall of words that share the common element.

In a part-to-whole approach, you would use this sequence:

(1) Display the prefix, suffix, or root word on the blackboard, in this case *un–.* Tell the children what it means (in this case, *not* or *the opposite of*).

(2) Prepare some 4 x 6 inch cards with root words that can be added to the prefix or suffix to make words. For root words, you will need to prepare cards with prefixes and suffixes on them. For example, for teaching *un–,* you would need cards that read *afraid, caged, ending, tangled.* For teaching the root word *cycle,* you would need cards that read *bi, tri, motor.* Add the cards to the element on the board and make new words.

(3) Finally, help the children put each newly-formed word into sentences, which can be written on the blackboard or on a piece of chart paper.

Synonyms and Antonyms

A good way to expand the meaning vocabularies of children is to teach lessons and play games with synonyms (two words with similar meanings) and antonyms (two words with different meanings).

One way to teach synonyms is to take five words, each with a clear synonym and write a paragraph that contains each of the five words. Highlight the five words. The paragraph will give children contextual clues to figure out the meanings of the five words if they don't know them. Then provide children with a "bank" of ten words, five of the words will be synonyms for the five target words, the other five will be words that are not synonyms for any of the five target words. Then challenge children to come up with synonyms for the highlighted words. You can use the same process to teach antonyms, just have the word bank include antonyms for the target words.

Once they have been introduced to word pairs that are either synonyms or antonyms, there are many games that children can play. In one, the teacher divides the class in half. She gives a word, written on a card, to each child. For each word, some child has a word that is a synonym (or an antonym if that is what the teacher is teaching). The children must then find their partner, the child who has the synonym for their word.

Using the Dictionary

Finally, children can learn the meanings of words by looking for a definition in a dictionary. There are a number of cautions to note here. First, be sure that children use a developmentally appropriate dictionary, one with appropriate words, a large enough typeface, child-friendly definitions, and plenty of illustrations. Second, there are problems with relying on the dictionary to find the meaning of a word. If you are reading and stop to consult a dictionary, the process is slow and distracts you from the meaning of whatever you are reading. When the children find the target word, they may not be able to understand the definition they read. If the word has more than one definition, the child may not know which definition is appropriate for the word, given the context of what he or she is reading. Before requiring children to use the dictionary, teachers should prepare them by ensuring they have learned certain dictionary skills: how to alphabetize words; how to recognize the differences in the alphabetical order of words that begin with the same letter(s); how to find and use guide words; and recognizing that word entries may have multiple definitions. Focus on the following:

* Understanding alphabetical order to the third, fourth, or fifth letter. You can't locate words in the dictionary unless you know how to alphabetize words.

* Using the guide words (first and last entry) that appear on each page of a dictionary. Efficient use of guide words will greatly facilitate the use of the dictionary.

* Considering the full definition of the word, and applying that definition to the target word in the context in which it appears. This is rather difficult, but simply finding the definition isn't enough, the child must consider the definition in relation to what he or she is reading.

* Dealing with multiple meanings. As an exercise, children should be given several words with multiple meanings (i.e., foul). Then they should be given sentences with different meanings of the word. For example: *Tucker hit a foul ball. There was a foul smell coming from the refrigerator.* Children should then match the appropriate dictionary meaning to each sentence.

Remember, it is important for teachers to first model the use of the dictionary, then provide students with a reasonable amount of guided practice in using the dictionary, and then challenge them to find meanings of words in the dictionary independently.

Chapter 13
Content Area 13:
Structure of the English Language

Introduction

This final content area is titled "Structure of the English Language." The RICA Content Specifications state that "structure of the English language refers to established rules for the use of the language. Students' knowledge of the structure of English promotes their reading fluency, listening and reading comprehension, and oral and written expression."

This content area incorporates the following things:

Sentence structure
Rules of English usage
Punctuation
Capitalization
Spelling (which was covered in Chapter 6)

The RICA Content Specifications also stress that K-12 students should understand that there are differences between spoken and written English and that direct, explicit instruction must be used to teach children the structure of the English language.

Definitions

Educators do not share a common definition for grammar. A definition linguists use is that grammar is a description of a language, including the sound system of that language (phonology), the system of creating words (morphology), the rules for forming sentences (syntax), and the nuances of word meaning (semantics). For our purposes, the word grammar means the rules of English. It is a broad term and includes sentence structure, punctuation, capitalization, and usage. In fact, if a teacher says he or she is teaching grammar, the lesson could include strategies for teaching any of those skills related to any of those four terms. The English-Language Arts Content Standards for California Public Schools consider the parts of speech (noun, verb, adjective, adverb, preposition, conjunction, interjection) to be a part of grammar.

Sentence structure refers to the rules of composing correct sentences in English. Not all combinations of words are correct and form sentences. For example, *The Oakland Raiders are going to win the Super Bowl this year* is an acceptable sentence in English. *Raiders are Super Bowl year this win to the Oakland the going* is not. There are a number of things that can be taught as a part of sentence structure: subject and predicate; incomplete and run-on sentences; simple, compound, and complex sentences; independent and dependent clauses.

A <u>clause</u> has a subject and a predicate. A clause that can stand alone as an acceptable sentence is an <u>independent clause</u> (i.e., *Darlene kicked the ball*). On the other hand, a clause that is not a complete thought is a <u>dependent clause</u> (i.e., in the sentence *Darlene kicked the ball to Fred, who kicked it to Allen*, the dependent clause is *who kicked it to Allen*).

A <u>simple sentence</u> has one independent clause (*Mr. Elgourach saw the white stag.*). A <u>compound sentence</u> is made up of two or more independent clauses (*He felt that he would be short forever and he tried to get used to it*). Complex sentences have one independent and one or more dependent clauses (*When he was awake, he was happy and sad at the same time.*).

<u>Usage</u> refers to correctness, or using the appropriate word or phrase in a sentence. Rules of proper usage will vary from dialect to dialect in English. Just think of all the different, but appropriate ways of saying certain phrases in London, England, from the way we say certain phrases here in California! Also, rules of usage vary from situation to situation. Choices of words and phrasing should be different, for example, if you are addressing the California Supreme Court or if you are talking to friends while watching Monday Night Football.

Examples of improper usage include using *catched* instead of *caught*; double subjects (*My mom she is a system analyst*); *hisself* for *himself*; or selecting the wrong pronoun (*Me and my friend went to the store*).

<u>Punctuation marks</u> and <u>capital letters</u> are two ways written English is different from spoken English. They must be used appropriately in written English, but they are inferred by the listener in spoken English.

It is important to note that in the <u>English-Language Arts Content Standards for California Public Schools</u>, this area of the curriculum is called "Written and Oral English Language Conventions."

How to Assess the Structure of the English Language

Samples of Student Writing

The most valid source of information about a student's knowledge of sentence structure, rules of usage, punctuation, and capitalization is the written text that a student produces during the school year. In other words, the real test is what students write. Thus, it is important for teachers to review and analyze the journal entries, stories, and essays students write during the school year. This type of assessment must be <u>ongoing</u> and conclusions should be reached only after analyzing <u>multiple</u> samples of student writing.

Teachers should use rubrics to organize their analysis (this was covered in Chapter 11). Again, teachers can analyze a piece of writing using multiple criteria (capitalization, punctuation) or a single criterion (proper sentence structure with no run-on sentences or sentence fragments).

Tests

Almost all of us have experienced tests of our knowledge of the structure of the English language. Most standardized tests of student achievement include a test of sentence structure, usage, punctuation, and capitalization. Most language arts textbook series have tests for students. Teachers can develop their own tests, but again, it is important to note that no test is a substitute for analyzing student writing. Some of the testing formats include:

The scrambled paragraph. Students are confronted with a paragraph with sentences out of order. They must put them in a proper order.

The naughty sentence. A common testing format is to present sentences to students that have been divided into four or five parts. One part of the sentence has an error in it (i.e., a usage error or missing punctuation). Students must identify the part of the sentence that is incorrect.

Choice of words. To test knowledge of usage, a sentence will have a missing word and students are presented with two or more choices (i.e., *who* or *whom*).

How to Teach the Structure of the English Language

There are significant differences of opinion about how to best teach the structure of the English language. There are disagreements over how much time should be devoted to this, or what precisely should be taught, or when certain topics should be covered. Questions of what and when have been resolved, to a large degree, by the English-Language Arts Content Standards for California Public Schools. At each grade level, there is a set of standards under the heading of "Written and Oral English Language Conventions" and there are subtopics for sentence structure, grammar (primarily teaching the parts of speech), punctuation, capitalization, and spelling.

The RICA Content Specifications take the position that the structure of the English language should be taught directly and explicitly.

Direct Lessons

Much of what has been presented so far in regards to the direct teaching of reading skills and strategies applies to the direct teaching of the structure of the English language. It is important to assess who needs each element you are teaching. For example, a fourth grade teacher likely will have many students who understand the use of question marks; she needs only teach a direct lesson on their use to those children who do not use them appropriately in their written work.

Teachers have many resources to choose from – there are lessons on the structure of English in basal reader workbooks and in the language arts textbooks that most school districts have purchased for classroom use.

A whole-part-whole approach would seem to work best when teaching sentence structure, punctuation, capitalization, parts of speech, and rules of English usage. For example, if the objective of a lesson is to teach students that the contraction *aren't* means *are not*, then the teacher should start by displaying sentences such as *Terri and Sonia aren't sisters but they look alike* and *Jason Giambi and Miguel Tejadaa aren't members of the San Francisco Giants, they play for the Oakland A's*. The teacher would then isolate the target contraction, circling *aren't* in each sentence. Then the teacher would explain that *aren't* is an abbreviated form of *are not*. Then, students would generate new sentences using *aren't*.

Individual Conferences

Teachers should have regular conferences with each student in their classroom to review the contents of the student's writing portfolio. While the first purpose of these conferences is to talk about the substance of what the student has written, teachers should also use the opportunity to teach mini-lessons on the structure of the English language. For example, a second grade teacher notices that a student continues to produce run-on sentences. The individual conference is a good time to show the child how his written work should be rewritten to include proper end punctuation.

Error Analyis

An activity used by many California elementary school teachers is some kind of daily exercise in analyzing grammatically incorrect sentences. The teacher displays a sentence on the blackboard that has three or four errors. Students are then challenged to rewrite the sentence so that it is correct. This is a good way for children to review what they have learned about the structure of the English language.

Language Activities to Build Knowledge of Academic Language

Teachers should plan and implement a variety of activities to help students master the use of "academic" language – the way of speaking and writing in school and most business settings.

Model. First of all, it is important that teachers continually provide a model of acceptable English usage when they speak and when they write.

Reading aloud content-area texts. Most teachers select narrative texts to read aloud to children (novels, picture book stories). To provide a model of expository text structures to children, teachers should read aloud from biographies, information books, social studies and science textbooks, newspapers, and magazines.

<u>Sentence expansion and combining</u>. In a sentence expansion activity, children are challenged to lengthen simple sentences. For example, the teacher writes the following sentence on the board: *The firefighter ran.* Then, the teacher asks students to describe the firefighter (*The tall, strong firefighter ran.*). Next, the teacher asks the students to consider why, where, and when the action is taking place (*The tall, strong firefighter ran into the burning building after she heard a person screaming.*).

A sentence combining activity involves taking two simple sentences and combining them into a compound sentence. For example, the teacher presents two sentences to her students: *Rich Gannon threw a pass to Tim Brown. Tim Brown ran to the 10-yard line.* The students would work to combine the sentences into one (there are many possibilities, like *Rich Gannon threw a pass to Tim Brown, who ran to the 10-yard line*).

Proofreading

Finally, another instructional activity that will help students enhance their understanding of the structure of the English language is proofreading. This is a significant challenge because students must <u>apply</u> what they have learned about sentence structure, punctuation, capitalization, and the rules of English usage. Students should be asked to proofread both their own work and papers written by their classmates. It probably is best to start with a proofreading exercise requiring an analysis for just one type of error (i.e., just look for punctuation errors).

Sample RICA Examination

You have four hours (240 minutes) to complete this examination.

Multiple Choice Section

Select the correct answer for each question.

1. A first grade teacher believes that she should read aloud to her students at least twice a day. She feels this will help her students develop:
a. A sense of how stories are constructed
b. An understanding of the proper spellings for diphthongs, like the *oi* in *oil*
c. Left to right directionality
d. The ability to proofread student-authored stories

2. Mr. Niyongabo teaches kindergarten. One key component of his reading/language arts program is the shared book experience. He will need:
a. Writing paper with clearly marked lines
b. 3 x 5 inch cards, each with one of the words on Fry's New Instant Word List
c. Big books
d. Students who have already developed the ability to read books written at a fourth grade instructional level

3. Mrs. Garcia teaches first grade. She has become frustrated with her attempts to use the Language Experience Approach (LEA) with her students. She does the LEA with some of her students in Spanish, which is their first language. For her English speakers, she does the LEA in English. She is frustrated because her students don't seem to say very much. Thus, she has little to write. This could be because:
a. For almost all of the LEA sessions, she insists on selecting the topics; for example, yesterday's topic was "Why should we work together to keep our classroom clean?"
b. Her students have not mastered the initial consonant sound-symbol relationships
c. Her students speak very little English
d. She doesn't use 10 x 14 inch newsprint paper with room at the top of each sheet for her students to illustrate what they have dictated

4. Mrs. Griffith teaches kindergarten. She has decided to construct a learning center featuring examples of environmental print. She will include all of the following <u>except</u>:
a. Old cereal boxes
b. Big books
c. Bumper stickers
d. Candy wrappers

5. Mr. Ribiero is a fifth grade teacher. Almost all of his students are excellent readers. He has four students, however, who have difficulty understanding what they read despite the fact that the children in this group make very few word identification errors. To help this group of four students, he should:

a. Develop a comprehensive plan to teach meaning vocabulary, especially key words this group of students will encounter in their basal readers, social studies, and science textbooks

b. Assess the students to determine if each has developed phonemic awareness; if not he should begin with a series of lesson on sound matching

c. Teach students to use guide words when they are using the dictionary

d. Do very little, there is every reason that this group of children will "outgrow" the problem with very little help

6. Ms. Junxia teaches fifth grade. She has five students who have difficulty with end punctuation. They sometimes omit any ending mark. But more frequently they use a period to end all sentences, even those requiring a question mark or an exclamation point. She has decided to teach this group of children a series of five lessons on end punctuation. Knowledge of the proper use of end punctuation affects reading performance because:

a. Students who know about how to use end punctuation appropriately will make fewer errors when asked to make up words with many prefixes and suffixes

b. This knowledge will reinforce their understanding that English moves left to right

c. End punctuation is only one aspect of knowing the structure of the English language

d. It will help students pause at appropriate places in the text and it will help them understand the meaning of the text

7. There are many words in the English language. Which words should a teacher select for meaning vocabulary lessons?

a. Words that are related to each other; words needed to comprehend a reading selection

b. The best idea is to proceed in alphabetical order. First, teach words that begin with A, then proceed to words that begin with B

c. Children must be taught the meanings of all words they don't know so the best way to proceed is to first ask children which words they would like to learn

d. There really is no way to decide which words to select for a meaning vocabulary lesson; perhaps the best idea is to use words that appear in a familiar document, like the menu from the school cafeteria

8. Mrs. Young is a first grade teacher. Six of her students are having difficulty learning the corresponding sounds that go with the consonants at the end of words. The first thing she should do for these students is:

a. Begin planning a series of direct, explicit lessons that will teach them consonant blends and consonant digraphs

b. Administer a test of concepts about print

c. Decide whether or not it is important for this group of children to be taught phonics

d. Do a thorough assessment to see if they can hear the individual sounds that occur at the end of words

9. Teachers with English Language Learners (ELLs) who are able to read in English will plan English reading activities for those students. How can teachers support the reading development of their ELLs?

a. Conduct daily assessment of each ELL on his or her ability to use morphemic analysis to decode difficult words

b. Understand that English differs from other languages in that not all languages are alphabetic and some languages are more phonetically regular than English

c. Understand that if the children have learned to read in a language other than English, that there will be a negative transfer of those literacy skills to English

d. Place the initial instructional emphasis on concepts about print, especially directionality and the tracking of English print

10. Miss Barrios is the principal at Shangri La School. Recent test results show that students at her school did poorly on phonics tasks. The primary grade teachers at her school agree that something must be done. As a first step, Miss Barrios should suggest that her teachers do which of the following:

a. Teach the rules of sound-symbol relationships by requiring children to restate those rules in language appropriate for their level of development

b. Work more on prefixes and suffixes, with emphasis on prefixes that negate (like *un*, *non*)

c. Conduct a thorough assessment of each child to determine precisely what sound-symbol relationships that each child knows and does not know

d. Ask students more questions that require critical thinking using materials designed for first, second, and third graders

11. Ms. Chung sang "Who has the /m/ word to share with us?" as her students looked at the stuffed animals she gave them. Fred, who had a monkey, said, "I do, Ms. Chung!" This is an example of:

a. A child who can successfully do sound matching tasks, and is developing phonemic awareness

b. A child who can successfully do sound addition and substitution tasks

c. A teacher who facilitates reading comprehension before students read, while they read, and after they read

d. A teacher who has successfully taught her students how to analyze literature by using the literary elements

12. Ms. Keino is a fourth grade teacher. She wants to increase the meaning vocabularies of her students. *In addition* to teaching her third grade students the meanings of difficult words they will read in their basal readers, social studies textbooks, and science textbooks, Ms. Keino should also:
a. Begin to use a direct and explicit approach to teaching phonics
b. Be sure that each student completes at least one workbook page a week
c. Do what is necessary to increase both the amount of time her students read and the types of books they read
d. Assess all her students for their ability to distinguish simple, compound, and complex sentences

13. A teacher who wants to increase the amount of time students spend reading independently has many possible instructional interventions to consider. If a teacher considers the possibilities and decides to administer an informal reading inventory (IRI), what is the rationale behind this choice?
a. An IRI has a high degree of validity because the inventory will include a battery of tests, each allowing the teacher to view reading development from a different perspective
b. In order to help children select books that are written at a level they can easily understand, it will be necessary to determine each child's independent reading level
c. Research shows that the amount of time any child spends reading independently depends on many factors
d. Student independent reading plays a critical role in promoting students' familiarity with language patterns

14. A shared book experience is a good way to teach concepts about print because:
a. The use of a big book will allow students to see the words on each page
b. When students dictate a story, they are using their own language
c. Phonemic awareness is a strong predictor of beginning reading success
d. Concepts about print are best learned from part to whole, rather than from whole to part

15. A fifth grade student is having difficulty with tasks requiring a search for information in a hard-cover encyclopedia. This student knows how to find the correct volume for the information she needs and she knows how to quickly locate the entry she is looking for. Her teacher notices, however, that she reads every word in the entry even when she only needs a single item of information. Her teacher should:
a. Require the student to only use online information sources because the hard-copy encyclopedia format will be obsolete in the near future
b. Further assess the student's vision because there is a very good chance that the difficulty is the result of poor eyesight
c. Teach the student to use the reading strategy of generating questions; this student will have no problems once she learns how to read the first paragraph of a content-area text and write a question that the remainder of the text will answer
d. Model and explicitly teach how to read for different purposes, especially how to scan for specific information

16. Ms. Wang has been using guided reading with a group of five of her students. The lessons always seem to go badly. The students in this group do not seem to understand what is going on in the stories they read. This could be because:

a. She should be doing guiding reading with her entire class, using an instructional aide to assist her less able readers

b. She neglected to include a writing assignment with each guided reading lesson; for example, writing personal responses to stories in journals

c. The five students have three different instructional reading levels

d. The five students are not all the same age

17. A teacher who selects high-frequency words for a weekly spelling list could provide the following rationale for that decision:

a. The use of morphemic analysis to decipher unknown words is an important skill for children to acquire and spelling lessons should focus on prefixes, suffixes, and root words

b. High-frequency words are those words that appear most frequently in printed English

ⓒ This will help children as they go about the process of mastering the most regular sound-symbol relationships in English

d. Phonetic spellers choose at least one letter to represent each sound in words they write

18. Mr. Kiptanui has a second grade student who has not learned the simple sound-symbol relationships that all second graders should know. He has taught his phonics lessons following a part-to-whole approach. He should now:

a. Rely on language play, requiring the student to memorize two or three simple chants each week

b. Assess his teaching, consider the alternatives, and try a whole-to-part-to-whole approach

c. Refocus on teaching the meanings of Greek and Latin root words

d. Realize that spelling instruction in context will teach the student most of the sound-symbol relationships he needs to know.

19. A fourth grade teacher in a small elementary school knows that both third grade teachers do a poor job of exposing their students to expository texts. A reasonable first step toward her goal of helping her students become proficient when reading such texts is to:

a. Include expository texts, like biography and information books, in her read aloud program

b. Develop a list of words that are likely to appear in the poetry she will read to her students; begin to directly teach the meanings of those words

c. Stop relying on standardized reading tests to make judgments about the reading ability of her students and start using a more comprehensive system of assessment

d. Acknowledge that learning in all content areas is supported by strong reading comprehension strategies and study skills

20. A teacher who decides to use onsets and rimes as a basis for a series of lessons for his students who are struggling with word identification could provide the following rationale for his decision:
a. Knowledge of onsets and rimes will help students understand story structure
b. It is easy to use diagrams, charts, and illustrations to teach onsets and rimes; this will particularly help the teacher's English Language Learners
c. Even though state and local content standards have inexplicably ignored onsets and rimes, standards produced by national organizations have emphasized their role in beginning reading instruction
d. Once a student understands the graphic representation for a rime, she has a useful tool to decode all words that include that rime

21. Ms. Yifter is a teacher who believes in a balanced approach to teaching reading. She understands the importance of phonemic awareness in reading development. So, she teaches many directed lessons to develop her kindergarteners' acquisition of phonemic awareness. To balance these lessons she should:
a. Develop a series of worksheets to reinforce what the students have learned
b. Administer a timed test to see what each student has learned
c. Use chants and songs with rhyming words
d. Use contextual redefinition and the clueing technique

22. Teachers should have an assessment plan that uses a variety of measures to evaluate student development. This would include informal measures like:
a. Anecdotal records the teacher has carefully kept while students are engaged in reading activities
b. A teacher-developed test of recognition of 100 high-frequency words
c. A standardized, norm-referenced test of reading comprehension if the test includes questions assessing the following levels of comprehension: literal, inferential, and evaluative
d. A test of concepts about print produced by the publisher of a basal reading series that includes a very specific script for the person administering the test

23. Miss Potenza would like her second graders to develop a sense of story structure. She thinks this will help them better understand the stories they read. She should:
a. Use story frames, and when students are ready, story grammars and story maps
b. Only use story grammars
c. Use guided reading lessons that focus on how different students can have different perspectives of the same event in a story
d. Use a combination of environmental print, the shared book experience, and read aloud

24. It is the sixth month of school and Mrs. Dombrowski is concerned. Five of her kindergarten students don't understand the words in a story are read left to right, top to bottom. She should:
a. Rely on environmental print, a print-rich environment, reading aloud, and shared book experiences to teach this concept
b. Refocus her attention on phonemic awareness
c. Use a variety of instructional strategies to teach her students to use context to decode words that they do not know
d. Plan and implement direct, explicit lessons to teach directionality

25. To teach the meanings of six words students will encounter in the story they will read in their basal readers, Mr. Young should first:
a. Prepare six copies of a worksheet; the worksheet will include three sentences for each of the words and attempt to teach their meaning through context
b. Prepare a chart listing the target words along the vertical axis and their characteristics along the horizontal axis
c. Give the students a simple test to determine which words each student does not know
d. Write the definitions of each word on six separate cards, but only display those cards if his oral explanations prove insufficient

26. Ms. Shuwei was a student teacher in a second grade classroom. She told her supervisor that the next time she visited she would teach a lesson on consonant blends. Ms. Shuwei was working on *ph* as in *graph*, *ch* as in *much*, and *sh* as in *bush*. She carefully told her students that these letter combinations made a blended sound, with each letter making a sound. Her supervisor had a shocked look on her face because:
a. Before students are able to learn about consonant blends, they must learn how to take turns when they work in small groups
b. These letters aren't consonant blends, they are consonant digraphs and each pair of letters makes only one sound
c. These letters aren't consonant blends, they are consonant diphthongs and each pair of letters makes a glided vowel sound
d. *Ph* as in *graph* and *ch* as in *much* should never be taught together in the same lesson

27. Mr. Borzov wanted his third grade students to know how to classify questions so they would be more efficient in locating answers. He agrees with the research that shows poor readers waste a great deal of time looking for the answers to questions that do not have an answer that can be found in one place in the text. He should:
a. Teach lessons that focus on the sound-symbol relationships of English because once students have improved their decoding abilities they will become more proficient readers
b. Be sure that he uses a pre-reading activity to activate background knowledge, like a KWL chart
c. Work on teaching inferential and evaluative comprehension skills and teach students the relationship between different types of questions and the locations of their answers
d. Begin each lesson with a CLOZE exercise

28. Mr. Berruti wants his fourth graders to use context to unlock the meanings of words they do not know. He will plan activities that will help his students use semantic clues, which are:
a. The meanings of surrounding words
b. Clues based on word order
c. Inappropriate for fourth graders because they are too easy
d. A part of morphemic analysis

29. Teachers should base their reading instruction on:
a. A sequence of reading skills provided by the teachers' edition of a basal reading system
b. State and local content and performance standards
c. The all-important goal of teaching children to use the public library
d. Story structure, through the use of story grammars, story maps, and story frames

30. Mrs. Rudolph teaches kindergarten. She regularly reads aloud books with wordplay, such as *Each Peach Pear Plum*. This should help her students acquire:
a. Phonemic awareness
b. Understanding of story structure
c. Use of affixes to recognize unknown words
d. A better knowledge of the importance of ongoing assessment using multiple sources

31. In order to meet the needs of a class of students with diverse abilities, a teacher should:
a. Develop a set of tests for each of the areas of reading development; for example, a kindergarten teacher should create tests for concepts about print, phonemic awareness, and word identification
b. Have children compare the properties of a set of words
c. Have children work in small groups to come up with responses to CLOZE passages
d. Use flexible grouping, individualized reading instruction, and timely intervention for those children having difficulty

32. *Chair, desk, fan*, and *shoe* are all examples of:
a. Free morphemes
b. Diphthongs
c. Bound morphemes
d. Words with two phonemes

33. Ms. Jacobs is a first grade teacher. She has assessed her students and determined that over half of them are at the pre-phonetic level of spelling development. To help these students become more accurate spellers she should:
a. Start by assessing the students' mastery of common prefixes and suffixes
b. Require the children to learn 15 sight words each week
c. Explicitly teach children the etymology of the 200 words that appear most frequently in printed English
d. Be sure the students have phonemic awareness; if they do, proceed to assess and teach phonics

34. Mrs. Kratzenberg teaches fifth grade. In her classroom there are seven English language learners who have an instructional reading level of grade three in English. During teacher-directed reading lessons, Mrs. Kratzenberg should:
a. Ask students to read aloud every day, without practice, and in random order
b. Be sure to use the comprehension questions that appear at the bottom of each page in the teachers' edition of the basal reader
c. Divide the lesson in three parts: First, teach basic literacy concepts, such as the directionality of English; second, focus on morphemic analysis, especially Greek and Latin root words; third, read through the story, stopping at the end of each paragraph to ask literal comprehension questions
d. Use a variety of strategies to support these students, including preview-review, visual aids, charts, and real objects

35. Knowledge of the proper use of punctuation marks helps make a reader more proficient because:
a. The structure of the English language refers to established rules for the use of language
b. Punctuation helps determine a text's meaning
c. Punctuation helps determine a text's length
d. The rules of English usage vary according to dialect

36. Ms. Romero teaches third grade. She wants to do a better job of selecting spelling words for her students to learn. She should:
a. Organize her spelling lists by grouping words by syllable length, and be sure that each week's list includes words of one, two, and three syllables
b. Find a list of the rimes that occur must frequently in printed English; then encourage her students to include words with those rimes in their entries in the their journals
c. Create lists of words based on orthographic patterns and high-frequency words that do not conform to those patterns
d. Realize that no systematic approach to teaching spelling works; that some children will always have difficulty with spelling

37. Most teachers have some students who devote little time to independent reading. To help these students read more, a teacher:
a. Needs to help them develop the ability to talk and listen informally
b. Must first help this group of students learn the names of the letters in the English alphabet
c. Should consider a variety of factors, including their knowledge of the rules of English usage
d. Should consider a variety of factors, including their reading interests and preferences

38. Mr. Nguyen is concerned about the difficulty many of his students have in reading their fourth grade social studies textbooks. He should:
a. Thoroughly assess the phonemic awareness of each student having difficulty
b. Teach a series of lessons on how to use the structure of expository text to improve comprehension
c. Teach several word identification strategies including phonics, sight words, and morphemic analysis
d. Realize the importance of narrative text structures and use those structures to help improve comprehension

39. When people write:
a. Purpose and audience should determine form
b. Form and audience determine purpose
c. Form and purpose determine audience
d. They should use the form they are most comfortable with, regardless of purpose

40. Mr. Jackson's second grade students draw as a pre-writing activity. While he believes this is a good way for young writers to organize their thoughts, he wants to expand their repertoire of pre-writing tools, so he could introduce:
a. The Yopp-Singer Test of Phonemic Segmentation
b. Skimming and scanning
c. Question-Answer Relationships
d. Quick Write

41. Fred, a third grade student, has completed a standardized, norm-referenced test of reading comprehension. He correctly answered 40 of the 50 questions on this exam. Which of the following would be reasonable set of scores for Fred:
a. A percentile score of 88 and a grade level equivalent score of 5.7
b. A percentile score of 88 and a grade level equivalent score of 1.7
c. A percentile score of 28 and a grade level equivalent score of 5.7
d. A percentile score of 28 and a grade level equivalent score of 1.7

42. On the graded reading passages of an informal reading inventory (IRI), a student's independent, instructional, and frustration reading levels are determined by:

a. Knowledge of sound-symbol relationships and performance on a spelling test

b. Percentage of oral reading miscues and percentage of correct answers to comprehension questions

c. Percentage of oral reading miscues and rate of reading

d. Number of words skipped divided by the number of words repeated

43. Miss Harris teaches fourth grade. She is teaching a series of lessons on the use of simile and metaphor in children's literature. This will help students better understand an author's use of:

a. Text structures that compare and contrast

b. Mood and tone

c. Figurative language

d. Integral setting

44. The stages (or phases) of the writing process are:

a. Drafting, editing/revising, publishing, redrafting

b. Prewriting, drafting, editing/revising, publishing

c. Experiencing, feeling, thinking, acting

d. Experiencing, prewriting, editing/revising, accepting

45. In order to assess spelling, a teacher should:

a. Use spelling tests and a standardized test of spelling

b. Ask students to orally spell words that the teacher dictates

c. Ask students to both write correctly and spell orally words that the teacher dictates

d. Use spelling tests and samples of student writing

46. Mr. Ramirez teaches sixth grade. He wants to determine who among his students will have difficulty with the sixth grade science book. He should:

a. Develop and administer tests of student knowledge of the etymology and morphology of specific "science" words

b. Use the following sources of information: the results of a standardized, norm-referenced reading comprehension test administered the year before; the results of an IRI; the results of a CLOZE test from the science textbook

c. Use the following sources of information: the results of a standardized, norm-referenced reading comprehension test administered the year before; the results of an IRI; the results of a test of word identification strategies

d. Randomly select fifty words from two pages in the middle of the science text; then ask each student to read the words aloud

47. Children in the precommunicative stage of spelling development:
a. Should have a program of reading instruction that focuses on learning sight words, especially the fifty words that appear most frequently in printed English
b. Will, for the most part, not want to take part in playful language activities, like chanting and singing
c. Do not use graphophonemic relationships when they write
d. Should have a program of reading instruction that focuses on phonics

48. A group of fifth grade students is having difficulty using commas appropriately in their writing. They use commas correctly with items in a series (i.e., *Salmon, tuna, and cod are all fish*) and when they write the date. Other than that, they rarely use a comma correctly. Their teacher should:
a. Develop and implement a series of teacher-directed lessons to teach the proper use of commas
b. Avoid calling attention to these errors so students maintain positive self-images as writers
c. Place the errors in context; as long as their written messages are comprehensible there is no need for concern
d. Develop and implement a series of teacher-directed lessons to teach the proper use of capital letters

49. A first grade teacher who wants to assess the reading comprehension of her students may decide to have her students retell a story they have read. This form of assessment will, in most cases, assess which of the following:
a. Literal comprehension of the story
b. Knowledge of high-frequency words
c. Inferential comprehension of the story
d. Knowledge of sound-symbol relationships

50. Once a teacher determines a child's level of spelling development, she should:
a. Find the relationship between that level and the child's instructional reading level
b. Work with the child to make sure the child does not overemphasize correctness
c. Attempt to help the child "move through" that level and on to the next
d. Rely on the lists of words provided by the spelling book

51. Mrs. Koolagonta wants to improve the reading comprehension of her students. She has assessed their different strengths and weaknesses. She has determined that six of her third graders do a good job of remembering the sequence and details of the stories they read, but they have difficulty when asked to summarize the main themes of these same stories. She should:

a. Develop and implement a series of lessons that focus on the contextual clues that unlock the meanings of unknown words

b. Conduct further assessment of this group of students to determine whether they are better at remembering story sequence or detail

c. Use multi-sensory teaching techniques, including kinesthetic and tactile approaches, to teach summarization

d. Begin by modeling the process of identifying possible themes and restating them in simple sentences

52. A first grade teacher who wants her students to know where to find the name of a book's author and title should:

a. Realize that there are many resources that can be used to teach these concepts about print, including the Language Experience Approach and environmental print

b. Assess each student, and then use student names as a basis of teaching these concepts

c. Assess each student, and then teach these concepts directly

d. Always point out the author and title when doing a shared book experience

53. A test of phonemic awareness could ask students to perform any of the following tasks: sound matching, sound isolation, sound blending, sound addition and substitution, and sound segmentation. Why might a teacher want to start with a test of sound segmentation?

a. A test of sound segmentation is easy to develop

b. This is the easiest of the phonemic awareness tasks

c. This is the most difficult of the phonemic awareness tasks

d. Because the other choice, to start with sound matching, requires the use of words with three and four syllables

54. After reading <u>Ella Enchanted</u>, a fifth grade boy writes the following in his journal: "This was a pretty good story. My sister, Asha, is smart and she is clumsy, just like Ella." This is an example of a student:

a. Not understanding what he has read

b. Analyzing the text using the literary elements

c. Making a personal connection with literature

d. Using genre as a basis for organizing a response

55. If an English Language Learner has first learned to read in her first language, what will positively transfer to the challenge of learning to read in English?
a. The directionality of printed text
b. The concept that print, in some form, carries meaning
c. The alphabetic concept
d. The meanings of some words; for example, the similarity of the Spanish *mi* and the English *my*

56. Mrs. Petrymyas has decided to use a semantic map to teach her children the meanings of three words they will encounter during a reading assignment in their social studies textbook. During the lesson, the students will:
a. Learn the difference between derivational and inflectional suffixes
b. Look at a list of attributes for the three words and then decide whether each attribute fits each word
c. Write each word in some sort of personal dictionary
d. Use diagrams to organize words and phrases that define each word

57. When reading expository text, students frequently will read "differently" than when they read a narrative text. They might, for example, have to skim or scan. This most likely would occur when a student:
a. Reads to locate information in an encyclopedia
b. Reads a chapter in a social studies textbook
c. Reads a biography of Marion Jones
d. Reads a poem written about Michael Johnson

58. Mr. Hana-Rigelman has used graphic organizers to provide students a preview of what they will be asked to read in social studies textbooks. They don't seem to be working. This could be because:
a. Each organizer consists of only three to five words
b. He has used the structure of the text to develop graphic organizers
c. He presents the graphic organizers to his students before they read
d. Each organizer is a chart summarizing what the content children learn when they read

59. Mrs. Kipkeni has five fifth grade students whose instructional reading level is fourth grade. She is determined that each of these students will meet the California *English Language Arts Content Standards* for grade five. She has:
a. Made a significant teaching error; the standards were never meant for every student
b. A poor understanding of the role standards are supposed to play; they were never meant to be the basis for how instruction is designed
c. A good understanding of the role standards play; they were meant for every student
d. Made a significant teaching error; the teachers' edition of the reading textbook series she uses will define what students should know and be able to do

60. Many teachers use onsets and rimes to improve the word identification skills of their students. This is because:

a. It makes sense to teach onsets and rimes because most young children are not ready to recognize the number of phonemes in a word

b. Once children know the definitions of *onset* and *rime*, they can determine which syllables have an onset and a rime and which only have a rime

c. Of all the word identification strategies children use, phonics is the least effective

d. The most common rimes appear repeatedly in English words

61. Mrs. Wang wants her seventh grade students to know to use morphemic clues to unlock the meanings of words they do not know. She should teach:

a. The importance of reading every word in a text

b. The meanings of Greek and Latin-based root words

c. How to increase reading fluency

d. How to divide words into syllables

62. Which of the following best describes a characteristic of effective phonics instruction:

a. It is child-centered: The instruction relies primarily on teaching sound-symbol relationships that children are most interested in learning

b. It is embedded: Most phonics instruction takes place as part of other language experiences

c. It is systematic: Instruction is sequenced according to the increased complexity of linguistic units

d. It is equitable: So that no child feels separated, all children should take part in each phonics lesson

63. A test of reading comprehension lacks *validity* if:

a. The percentage of correct answers for the mean student is less than 10% greater than the mean percentage of correct answers for the lowest performing students in the sample group

b. The test measures something else besides reading comprehension

c. The test fails to measure word identification as well

d. Different forms of the test provide consistent results

64. The following principles should guide your assessment of your students:

a. Assessment should be ongoing; you should gather information from multiple sources

b. The most important information is the students' self assessment

c. Tests should have both multiple choice and essay questions; tests should be brief

d. No formal test measures everything, so the key is to use many different formal tests, each with high reliability and validity

65. Mrs. Bazile is the principal of E. B. White Elementary School. She visited a second grade classroom and met with the teacher after school. Mrs. Bazile told the teacher, "I was so impressed with how you have organized your classroom library. You really have made it easy for students to find books that they are able to read." The teacher might have:

a. Restricted access to the classroom library so that students only go there when the teacher or an instructional aide can assist them in selecting a book

b. Prepared a bulletin board next to the classroom library featuring the last ten winners of the Caldecott Medal

c. Chosen only 50 books for the library; for each book she has highlighted in yellow the words that last year's students could not identify

d. Organized the books by independent reading level

66. At the beginning of the school year, teachers should complete an IRI for each of their students. The IRI will include graded reading passages, students will read aloud several of these passages. The teacher will complete a miscue analysis of these oral reading episodes. Why?

a. Students enjoy reading aloud; there are many tests in an IRI and it is important that the testing process include some activities the children find enjoyable

b. All California children are required to take reading tests in the spring of each year; these tests all include oral reading

c. The miscue analysis will reveal which children are able to answer evaluative comprehension questions

d. The analysis provides information needed to determine each child's instructional reading level

67. Mr. Assiz is a kindergarten teacher. He wants his students to develop an understanding of word boundaries, which is knowing:

a. The number of letters in a word

b. The configuration of words (i.e., their "shape")

c. Where one word ends and another begins

d. The first and last sound of a word

68. A fourth grade student reads aloud at a pace that is too fast. Further, he fails to pause at appropriate places in the text. His teacher should:

a. Model reading at an appropriate pace and with appropriate pauses; then have the student practice in individualized sessions

b. Teach the student the meaning of words with three and four syllables

c. Always ask the student to retell what he or she has read

d. Be thankful, the real problem is when students read too slowly

69. "Strategic" readers choose to implement a variety of interventions when they are reading. These include:
a. The ability to distinguish characters from setting
b. Use of the library to find specific details
c. The use of phonemic awareness to segment words
d. Stopping to clarify, perhaps by rereading a paragraph

70. Mr. Chin is a fifth grade teacher. He has tested a student and learned that this student has very poor word identification skills. In fact, the student struggles with consonant blends, consonant digraphs, and diphthongs. Mr. Chin should:
a. Teach this student those sound-symbol relationships
b. Focus on fifth grade word identification tasks, like learning the meanings of common Greek and Latin root words
c. Place the student in a second grade classroom during reading time
d. Work on skimming and scanning, important content-area reading skills for fifth grade

Focused Educational Problems and Instructional Tasks

Number One

Answer the following in approximately 50 words.

Use the information below to complete the exercise that follows.

Mr. Lopez is a first grade teacher. He has 19 students. Mr. Lopez wants to administer an informal reading inventory to each of students. The IRI will include graded word lists and graded word passages. He is not sure what other types of tests to include.

Examinee Task

Using your knowledge of reading assessment, select two other types of tests that Mr. Lopez should include in his first grade IRI. Explain why each one should be administered.

Number Two
Answer the following in approximately 50 words.

Use the information below to complete the exercise that follows.

Ms. MacDowell teaches fourth grade. She has six students who are English language learners. Four are native Spanish speakers and two are native Cantonese speakers. All have made good progress in acquiring oral English. The results of an IRI in English showed that all three of the students have an instructional reading level of grade three and three of the ELLs have a much lower instructional reading level, grade one.

Examinee Task

How should Ms. MacDowell organize the reading instruction she provides for these six students?

Number Three
Answer the following in approximately 150 words.

Use the information below to complete the exercise that follows.

Mrs. Tamas is a sixth grade teacher. She has four students whose instructional reading level is grade five. This group of students shares a common reading preference: they all like reading comic books. These students do okay when they read from their sixth grade basal readers, but they are having difficulty with their social studies and science textbooks.

Examinee Task

Describe two things Mrs. Tamas can do to help these students better understand their social studies and science textbooks. Explain why each intervention will help.

Number Four
Answer the following in approximately 150 words.

Use the information below to complete the exercise that follows.

Mrs. Oglesby's first grade class includes a student, Peyton, who is having a great deal of difficulty with reading tasks. A look at Peyton's cumulative record reveals that he missed 65 school days in kindergarten due to injuries he suffered in a automobile accident (he is fine now). He thought there were three sounds in the following words: *at, boo,* and *elephant.* Peyton could not identify rhyming pairs of words. He could not identify the author and the title of a book Mr. Oglesby read to him. When Mrs. Oglesby asked Peyton to help her read the book, he seemed to have no idea what to do when he came to the end of a line.

Examinee Task

Based on the information provided, identify two areas of reading development that are crucial for Peyton. Then, for each area, describe one type of instructional activity that will help Peyton become a more proficient reader.

Case Study

This case study focuses on Julie, who is seven years old and in the second grade. Her primary language is English. Her health is fine, her vision and hearing have been tested and are normal. She tries her best in school. The documents on the following pages describe Julie's reading performance during the middle of the school year (in January, traditional calendar). Using these materials, write a response in which you apply your knowledge of reading assessment and instruction. Your response should include three parts:

(1) Identify three of Julie's reading strengths and/or needs at this point in the school year, citing evidence from the documents to support your conclusions;

(2) Describe two specific instructional strategies and/or activities designed to foster Julie's literacy development for the remainder of the school year by addressing the needs and/or building on the strengths you identified; and

(3) Explain how each strategy/activity you describe would promote Julie's reading proficiency.

Test of Letter Recognition

The 26 letters of the alphabet were arranged randomly. Julie was asked to read them. She read all the letters correctly. Score: 26/26.

Informal Reading Assessment

Printed below is the record Julie's teacher made of her oral reading. Julie was asked to read aloud the selection. As Julie read, the teacher kept a record of her performance. This is a first grade passage from the *Bader Reading and Language Inventory* (3rd ed.).

Pat and the Kitten

Pat saw a kitten. It was on the side of the street. It was sitting under a blue car.

"Come here, little kitten," Pat said. The kitten looked up at Pat. It had big yellow eyes. Pat took her from under the car. She that her leg was hurt.

"I will take care of you." Pat said. She put her hand on the kitten's soft, black fur.

"You can come home with me."

The kitten gave a happy *meow*.

Teacher's notes: 80 words, 7 errors. Julie does not pause when she sees a comma and she does not stop when she comes to the end of a sentence. She reads as if the punctuation was not there.

Key: ◯ deletion | short pause   ← repetition

     Ⓒ self-correction || long pause   CAT/cow substitution

     ⊤ teacher provided the word after a long pause

Julie's teacher let Julie read the selection silently. Then she asked Julie to retell the story. Below is a record of the items she mentioned during this unaided recall.

- ✓ Pat saw a kitten
- ✓ on the side of a street/under a car
- ___ come here, Pat said
- ___ kitten looked up
- ✓ big yellow eyes, black fur
- ___ her leg was hurt
- ✓ I will take care of you
- ___ Pat put hand on fur
- ✓ come home with me
- ✓ kitten meowed happily

Score: __6__/10

Results of Phonics Tests

Julie was asked to read lists of words.

Initial consonants	9/10	(missed word with initial *s*)
Initial blends	8/10	(missed *st* in *stay* and *spr* in *spring*)
Digraphs	6/10	(missed words starting with *ph*, *ch*)
Ending sounds	8/10	(didn't say *s* in *plants*, read *bet* for *beach*)
Medial Vowels	8/10	(read *met* for *meet* and *did* for *dead*)

Test of Basic Sight Words

In a test of 50 basic sight words (selected randomly from Fry's 240 "Instant Words"), Julie correctly identified 42 of the 50 words. She missed: *know, because, again, away, thought, beginning, together, took.*

Interest Inventory

The teacher read the questions, Julie gave her answers orally:

Think of all the things we do in our classroom. Think about everything from when we get here in the morning until we leave at night. What do you like best? *Mmmmm, that's hard. I like when we go outside and play games. I also like to act in plays.*

Do you have a favorite book? *Yes. It's the book you read to us yesterday about the grandfather from Japan. He went back to Japan.*

If you could do anything you wanted for one hour, what would it be? *That's easy. I would play soccer and then go swimming.*

Do you have a favorite movie? *Yes. I like "The Little Mermaid." My grandma gave it to me last year for my birthday.*

Do you read at home? *A little, when I don't have anything else to do. Well, actually my big sister who is in the other school likes to read to me. But not as much as she you used to. My mom and dad watch television more.*

Answers to the Sample Examination

Multiple Choice

1. A   Reading aloud will provide children with an understanding of story structure.

2. C   Shared book experiences require the use of a big book.

3. A   If the teacher selects the topics for LEA sessions, then many children will have little, if anything, to say. Children should select most of the topics to stimulate their dictation.

4. B   Big books are not environmental print. Environmental print includes those texts which are not produced for educational purposes.

5. A   None of the other choices make sense. There are several things Mr. Ribiero could do, and teaching meaning vocabulary is one of them.

6. D   Punctuation requires pauses and stops. To understand most texts, the reader must understand the role punctuation marks play.

7. A   Meaning vocabulary lessons work best if the words are related to the same topic. Words that are essential to understanding a story also are good choices for vocabulary lessons.

8. D   If first graders routinely have difficulty with sounds at the end of words, it is a good idea to do a phonemic awareness test, to be sure they are aware of those sounds.

9. B   If ELLs have learned to read in the first language, then there will be both positive and negative transfer to the challenge of reading in English. Those languages that are alphabetic will have the most positive transfer, though some students who have learned to read in languages that have a higher degree of phonetic regularity than English will face some real frustration.

10. C   Thorough assessment is the first step to improving phonics instruction at this hypothetical school.

11. A   This was a sound matching task, a part of acquiring phonemic awareness.

12. C   This is an issue of balance. In addition to the direct, explicit vocabulary teaching Ms. Keino will do, she must balance that instruction with a plan to increase the independent reading of her students.

13. B   To connect children to appropriate books, the teacher would need to know the independent reading levels of her students.

14. A   The power of the shared book experience is that students can see the text, thus concepts about print like directionality and word boundaries can be taught.

15. D   This student needs to know how to read quickly until she finds what she is looking for.

16. C Guided reading lessons require that students be grouped by their instructional reading levels.

17. B Because they appear so often in printed English, high-frequency words are a good choice for inclusion on a spelling list.

18. B If one approach to teaching phonics directly and explicitly doesn't work, the teacher should try another.

19. A A teacher who wants to introduce her students to expository texts should select information books, biographies, and encyclopedia entries to read to her students.

20. D Rimes are a good thing to know because a common rime appears in many English words (like the *at* in *bat, cat, rat,* etc.).

21. C Again, a question of balance. These direct, explicit lessons should be balanced with lighthearted activities with rhyming words, like chants and songs.

22. A The other options are formal assessments.

23. A Story frames, story grammars, and story maps are all devices teachers use to teach story structure.

24. D At this point, direct intervention is necessary.

25. C Although many teachers do not have the time they need to do all the assessment they would like to, the correct answer is that before teaching any group of children a set of words, the teacher should determine which children already know which words.

26. B The supervisor was shocked because Ms. Shuwei didn't know the difference between consonant blends and consonant digraphs.

27. C Students can be taught the differences among literal, inferential, and evaluative questions and how to answer each type of question.

28. A Semantics refers to word meaning.

29. B Instruction should be based on our California standards and, if they exist, local school district standards.

30. A Alliteration helps students acquire phonemic awareness.

31. D In almost any classroom there will be children with widely different reading abilities. From an organizational standpoint to meet the needs of diverse students, teachers must use flexible grouping, individualized instruction, and intervention with children's particular difficulty.

32. A They are words without prefixes or suffixes, so they are free morphemes.

33. D Pre-phonetic spellers do not assign at least one letter to each sound in a word. The first step is to determine if they recognize all the sounds in words.

34. D This menu of strategies can provide the "scaffolding" necessary in a reading lesson with English language learners.

35. B Punctuation helps determine a text's meaning.

36. C   Spelling lists should include both words that follow the orthographic patterns of English (like *date, hope, time*) and those "outlaw" words that do not (*love*).

37. D   Reluctant readers need to be connected with books written about topics they prefer.

38. B   Text structure, like compare and contrast, can be used to prepare graphic organizers and study guides.

39. A   Purpose and audience determine the written form a writer selects.

40. D   A quick write is a simple pre-writing activity.

41. A   It is impossible to determine precisely what percentile and grade equivalent scores would be assigned to Fred. It would all depend on the previous performance of the sampling group. A percentile score of 88 and grade level equivalent score of 5.7 seems about right.

42. B   Two factors determine reading levels on an IRI: number of miscues and number of questions answered correctly.

43. C   Simile and metaphor are examples of figurative language

44. B   The stages are: pre-writing, drafting, editing/revising, and publishing

45. D   To assess spelling, use both tests and samples of student writing

46. B   It is important to include the use of a CLOZE test.

47. C   Pre-communicative spellers use symbols other than letters and their choice of letters is random in that the letters do not represent sounds.

48. A   It is time to teach this group of students how to use commas.

49. A   Retellings assess literal comprehension.

50. C   The goal of spelling development is to help children progress through the stage they are in and move on to the next stage.

51. D   The best way to begin to teach summarizing is for the teacher to model it through "think alouds."

52. C   First assess, then teach to those who have not acquired this concept about print.

53. C   If a child can segment words, that is, identify how many sounds are in a word and name those sounds, then the chances are that she can complete the other, simpler phonemic awareness tasks.

54. C   Recognizing a link between a living person and a fictional character shows the student has made a personal connection with the book.

55. B   Regardless of the language a student first learned to read in, the student will have acquired the concept that print, in some form, is used to transmit meaning.

56. D   Semantic maps are diagrams.

57. A   When reading an encyclopedia, efficient readers skim and scan.

58. A   Graphic organizers will, in almost every case, require more than three to five words.

59. C   All students are expected to achieve California's grade level standards.

60. D   The most common rimes do appear frequently in English words.

61. B   Morphemic analysis uses prefixes, root words, suffixes, compound words.
62. C   Phonics instruction should be systematic in that instruction progresses from the simple sound-symbol relationships to the more complex.
63. B   A test is valid if it measures what it claims to measure.
64. A   Assessment should be ongoing and gather data from multiple sources.
65. D   A library organized by independent reading levels will help students find books they are able to read.

66. D   A miscue analysis of oral reading must be performed to find independent, instructional, frustration reading levels.
67. C   Word boundaries show where words start and finish.
68. A   To help this student, the teacher needs to model appropriate reading paces and monitor the student's progress in individual sessions.
69. D   Strategic readers know when they are confused. They stop and do something to clarify the text's meaning.
70. A   This fifth grader must learn these basic sound-symbol relationships.

How well did you do on the Multiple Choice section?

On the real RICA there will be 70 multiple choice questions. Remember, though, that only 60 are scored. The other ten are experimental. You won't know which ten questions don't count, so answer every question. It takes a score of 81 to pass RICA, so you should get at least 40 of the 60 multiple choice questions correct (66.7%). On our sample RICA, let's count all 70 of the multiple choice questions. You should have answered 47 of the 70 correctly (67.1%). Please note, though, that my questions may be easier than the ones you will answer when you take the RICA, and some may be more difficult.

Focused Educational Problems and Instructional Tasks

Question One

Sample Answer

The teacher should select a test of phonemic awareness and a series of phonics tests. The Yopp-Singer Test of Phonemic Segmentation would be a good choice. The phonics tests would ask children to decode words with common sound-symbol elements, like initial consonant blends. These tests will provide very specific information about each child's strengths and weaknesses.

It is important to include a test of phonemic awareness because first graders should have the ability to recognize the discreet sounds of English. Phonemic awareness provides a foundation for successful phonics teaching. For phonics instruction to be efficient, the teacher must know which children need to work on which sound-symbol relationships.

<u>Assessing Your Answer</u>

Assessing your own essay answers will be difficult. I suggest you exchange papers with someone who is in the credential program with you. For the short essays, two assessors will read your answer and give from 0 – 3 points. Their scores will be added together. So, your total score will be from 0 – 6.

To score your answer to this question, give yourself three points if you mentioned any of the following: concepts about print, phonemic awareness, phonics, sight words. Including tests of any of these four things would be correct. Only give yourself a 3 if you mentioned two types of tests <u>and</u> explained why you selected them. Finally, multiply your score by 2. Total possible is 6.

Question Two

<u>Sample Answer</u>

Because the students have instructional reading levels two grades apart, Mrs. MacDowell should divide the students into two groups for guided reading lessons. She should use flexible grouping to teach the students the reading skills they need (like knowledge of sight words). It is possible that some groups will include children from both groups. Finally, she should provide individualized instruction to any child who is having particular difficulty.

<u>Assessing Your Answer</u>

The key is that children who have instructional reading levels this far apart must be separated into two groups for many activities, especially guided reading lessons that attempt to teach comprehension skills. You should also mention flexible, needs-based groups, and the need for timely, individualized intervention with those children who are struggling. Give yourself three points if you mentioned each of these three grouping formats. Don't forget to multiply your score by two. Total possible is 6.

Question Three

<u>Sample Answer</u>

Mrs. Tamas should use expository text structures to help this group of students improve their comprehension of content-area. These structures include compare and contrast, cause and effect, chronological listing, problem and solution, and description. She can use the structure of a chapter in the social studies text, for example, to create a graphic organizer of the chapter. This would provide the students with a preview of the chapter's important ideas.

Expository texts, like social studies and science textbooks, are written differently from narrative texts. Knowledge of the structure of an expository text can help a reader understand the information the text is attempting to transmit.

The question provides information about the independent reading habits of this group of four students. They read comic books. Another intervention Mrs. Tamas should try would be to get these students to read independently expository texts, like biographies and information books.

This would help their comprehension of content-area textbooks in two ways. It would provide exposure to the style of expository writing and it would provide essential background information the students can draw upon to understand concepts in social studies and science.

Assessing Your Answer

There are many possible instructional interventions the teacher could use. Give yourself credit for the two I chose, text structures and independent reading of expository texts. You could have chosen lessons on inferential and evaluative comprehension, perhaps by using the QARs. You could have mentioned lessons on strategic reading, emphasizing the ability to predict, clarify, and summarize. Finally, you could have written about teaching vocabulary lesson focusing on the difficult words the students will read in their social studies or science textbooks.

These longer-answer essay questions are graded by two assessors, each giving your answer from 0 to 3 points. Their scores are added and then multiplied by two. There are 12 possible points on the longer-answer essays. These are "weighted," they are twice as important as the shorter-answer questions. For your score on this question, give yourself from 0 to 3 points, and since you are the only person who graded it, you will need to multiply that score by 4. Total possible is 12.

Question Four

Sample Answer

Perhaps because he missed so many days of kindergarten, Peyton lacks concepts about print and phonemic awareness. His inability to identify authors and titles on book covers and his lack of sense of the directionality of English indicate he lacks at two important concepts about print. His inability to identify the number of sounds in two and three-sound words and his problems with rhyming words reveal a lack of phonemic awareness.

While it is possible that Peyton will acquire some concepts about print through activities like shared book experiences, Mrs. Oglesby needs to teach him the concepts he lacks directly and explicitly. To teach book orientation, she will plan individualized instruction. Mrs. Oglesby can use picture books she has read to class. With Peyton, she will point out the author and title on the cover of each book. Eventually, she will challenge Peyton to make these identifications as he selects books to read independently.

To teach phonemic awareness, Mrs. Oglesby may want to start with a simple task, like identifying words that rhyme. She will need to teach this in one-to-one sessions unless there are other children in her room who share this need. During such a lesson, Mrs. Oglesby would say pairs of words, some which rhyme (*date, late*) and some that don't (*hope, pop*). Peyton would be challenged to identify those pairs that rhyme.

Assessing Your Answer

No wiggle room here. The two areas Peyton needs to work on are concepts about print and phonemic awareness. While he undoubtedly lacks phonics skills and knowledge of many high-frequency words, the question doesn't mention either area.
Only give yourself three points if you identified concepts about print and phonemic awareness and described one way to teach each area. Again, multiply your score by 4. Total possible is 12.

Case Study

Sample Answer

Strengths and Weaknesses

Julie has made considerable progress as a reader. She knows all her letters. She read the first grade passage with over 90% accuracy and with 60% comprehension, so her instructional reading level is first grade. While she is not reading at grade level, neither is she a non-reader. Three areas of weakness are:

Knowledge of punctuation marks and how they impact reading fluency. The teacher's notes reveal a significant issue here. Julie doesn't pause when she sees a comma and she doesn't stop at the end of sentences. It is somewhat surprising her comprehension score was as high as it was because failure to "read" punctuation can obscure a passage's meaning.

Word identification strategies, specifically phonics. The specific tests the teacher administered shows Julie needs to complete her knowledge of sound-symbol relationships. The results of the oral reading of the first grade selection and the tests reveal she has problems with *s* sounds. On the graded passages she could not identify *side, street, sitting*, and *soft*. She also needs to master two-letter combinations. She had trouble with the consonant digraphs *ph* and *ch* and she missed two-vowel combinations in the words *meet* and *dead*.

Independent reading. Julie would benefit greatly if she would increase the amount of time she reads on her own. This will improve her vocabulary and comprehension. The results of the survey showed she likes to play outside (soccer, swimming) and that she only reads when she has 'nothing else to do."

<u>Two Instructional Strategies/Activities</u>

<u>Participation in Reader's Theater: Fluency/Punctuation</u>. In the survey, Julie said "I also like to act in plays." Julie's teacher should include Julie in several reader's theater productions. She reads well enough to be successful in presentations based on simple picture books. During rehearsals, Julie's teacher should emphasize pausing when the text has a comma and stopping when she comes to the end of a sentence.

<u>Direct Phonics Lessons: Word Identification</u>. The results of the tests show that Julie needs direct, explicit instruction on the sound-symbol relationships she has not yet learned. There is a good chance that there are other children in Julie's classroom who share this need, so Julie's teacher can use flexible grouping patterns to work with Julie and the other students. A good place to start would be with *s* in the initial position. Then, *s* in the ending position. The lesson could then move to her other needs. Given the number of words she does know, it might be best for her teacher to start with lessons following a whole-to-part (analytic) format.

<u>Why Each Strategy/Activity Will Help</u>

A good way to teach children the meaning of punctuation marks is through drama. Reader's theater requires repeated readings of the same text, usually after a model provided by the teacher. Repeated readings completed at an appropriate pace, with appropriate pauses and stops, and with proper inflection are a good way to improve reading fluency. Julie likes dramatic activities so she should do well.

Children who have not acquired the sound-symbol relationships appropriate for their grade level need to be taught them directly. The type of lessons described above are based on a thorough assessment of her specific needs. The whole-to-part format would seem best for a student who already knows many words.

Assessing Your Answer

Your answer to the case study is read by two assessors, each gives you from 0 to 4 points. Their scores are added and then multiplied by 3! Your total possible score is 24.

<u>Strengths and Weaknesses</u>: In addition to what I mentioned you could have written about Julie's sight vocabulary. It is both a strength, in that she correctly identified 42 of the 50 words, and a weakness in that she missed some fairly easy words. Her retelling was relatively good, but I don't think there is enough there to classify her comprehension abilities. Do not give yourself 4 points unless you cited specific evidence from the case study in this part of your answer.

<u>Instructional Strategies/Explanation</u>. There really are dozens of possibilities here. You could have written about ways to improve her sight vocabulary. You could have

addressed ways to increase her independent reading. Another choice would have been a description of the direct teaching of end punctuation marks.

Assess your answer for clarity. Was each part of your answer clearly labeled? The question only asked for three strengths/weaknesses. If you wrote about many more, don't give yourself a 4. If you neglected to explain why your instructional strategies would work, only give yourself a 2. In any case, give yourself a score from 0 to 4 and then multiply your score by 6. Total possible is 24.

Your Total Score

Multiple Choice	_____	correct of 70
Essay One	_____	of 6 possible points
Essay Two	_____	of 6 possible points
Essay Three	_____	of 12 possible points
Essay Four	_____	of 12 possible points
Case Study	_____	of 24 possible points
Total	_____	of 130 possible points

Once again, the real RICA has 120 points and it takes 81 to pass (67.5%). Our test counted all 70 of the multiple choice questions, so it has 130 points. A passing score on this 130-point test would be 88. Please remember that this sample test may be easier than the RICA you take or it might be more difficult.

Good luck!

Appendices

Appendix

Appendix A

Student Name _____ Highest instructional level (2w) _____

A	B	C	D
(PP)	(P)	(1.0)	(2.0)
____ the	____ come	____ today	____ biggest
____ am	____ you	____ does	____ where
____ get	____ went	____ three	____ yourself
____ is	____ him	____ from	____ those
____ and	____ two	____ under	____ before
____ here	____ then	____ began	____ things
____ see	____ know	____ name	____ stopped
____ not	____ around	____ there	____ place
____ can	____ pet	____ could	____ always
____ will	____ house	____ again	____ everyone

E	F	G	H
(3.0)	(4.0)	(5.0)	(6.0)
____ morning	____ important	____ because	____ aircraft
____ since	____ airport	____ bridge	____ necessary
____ together	____ through	____ microscope	____ argument
____ begin	____ fifteen	____ curious	____ chemical
____ which	____ information	____ estimation	____ representative
____ near	____ ocean	____ reliable	____ terminal
____ should	____ preview	____ government	____ apology
____ yesterday	____ laughter	____ business	____ instruction
____ eight	____ preparation	____ direction	____ evidence
____ remember	____ building	____ avenue	____ consideration

From Lois A. Bader, *Bader Reading and Language Inventory* (3rd ed.), p. 13. Columbus, OH: Merrill/Prentice Hall, 1998. Reprinted with permission.

Appendix B

Student Name _Valerie_   Highest instructional level (2w) _/_
Grade : 1

A	B	C	D
(PP)	(P)	(1.0)	(2.0) _BAGGEST_
✔ the	✔ come	✔ today	___ biggest _C_
✔ am	✔ you	✔ does	✔ where
✔ get	✔ went	✔ three	✔ yourself
✔ is	_HIT_ ___ him _C_	✔ from	✔✔ those
✔ and	✔ two	(under)	✔ before
✔ here	✔ then	✔ began	✔ things
✔ see	_KA-NŌ_ ___ know	✔ name	_STEPPED_ ___ stopped
✔✔ not	✔✔ around	✔ there	✔✔ place
✔ can	✔ pet	_COLD_ ___ could	(always) _AIRYONÉ_
✔ will	✔ house	✔ again	___ everyone

✔ CORRECT   ✔✔ HESITATES   C SELF-CORRECTION
⬭ COULDN'T SAY

E	F	G	H
(3.0)	(4.0)	(5.0)	(6.0)
___ morning	___ important	___ because	___ aircraft
___ since	___ airport	___ bridge	___ necessary
___ together	___ through	___ microscope	___ argument
___ begin	___ fifteen	___ curious	___ chemical
___ which	___ information	___ estimation	___ representative
___ near	___ ocean	___ reliable	___ terminal
___ should	___ preview	___ government	___ apology
___ yesterday	___ laughter	___ business	___ instruction
___ eight	___ preparation	___ direction	___ evidence
___ remember	___ building	___ avenue	___ consideration

137

TONY AND THE FLOWER SHOP

Tony lived in a big city. He ran a flower shop. Tony loved his flowers, for the flowers did not make any noise. Tony loved peace and quiet.

The city where Tony lived was noisy. The buses, trucks, and cars were very noisy. He did not like the noise of the city.

Without the quiet Tony found in the flower shop, he would have moved from the city. The flower shop was his only reason for staying in the city.

From Lois A. Bader, *Reader's Passages to accompany Bader Reading and Language Inventory* (3rd ed.), p. 8. Columbus, OH: Merrill/Prentice Hall, 1998. Reprinted with permission.

CONSTELLATIONS

People all over the world have looked at the stars and have seen patterns that reminded them of everyday things. A group of stars that forms such a pattern is a constellation. A constellation lies within a definite region of the sky. By knowing the positions of the constellations, one can locate stars, planets, comets, and other galaxies. There are eighty-eight officially recognized constellations.

Many of the ancient names for certain constellations are still used today, though the things they were named for are no longer a part of our everyday experiences.

Almost anyone who grew up in the Northern Hemisphere can point out the Little Dipper. The Little Dipper is part of the constellation Ursa Minor, which means Little Bear.

Ursa Minor appears to circle the North Star. It is visible all year long. Some groups of stars are only visible during certain seasons of the year.

There are twelve seasonal constellations that are especially important because the sun and the moon always rise within one of their patterns. These are the constellations of the Zodiac.

Constellations are used in ship and airplane navigation. Astronauts use them to help orient spacecraft.

From Lois A. Bader, *Reader's Passages to accompany Bader Reading and Language Inventory* (3rd ed.), p. 23. Columbus, OH: Merrill/Prentice Hall, 1998. Reprinted with permission.

Substitution and mispronunciations
Underline and write the student's response above the word

Example: they <u>will</u> go to principal's office

(handwritten above "will": shall)

Repeated word
Underline and write "R" above the word or phrase that was repeated

Example: Fred decided to go <u>to the movies</u>.

(handwritten above "to the movies": R)

Insertions
Write the word the student inserted with a caret

Example: the ^ bear

(handwritten above caret between "the" and "bear": big)

Omissions
Circle the word omitted

Example: and so the (grumpy) giant walked

Words provided by the person giving the test
Underline the word and write T above it

Example: was so heavy it took three <u>sailors</u> to lift it

(handwritten above "sailors": T)

Self-corrections by the student
Underline the word, write the word the student said first, then write a C

Example: the <u>terrible</u> storm destroyed

(handwritten above "terrible": terrific C)

Appendix F   Scoring Sheet — Graded Reading Passage

Student's Name ___Debbie___ Date _11/21/00_

Passage Level: 3

JAMES' CUT

It was after lunch when James cut his finger on the playground. He was bleeding

HURTING

and he hurt a little too.

R

He went inside to find his teacher. He showed her his cut finger and asked for

R

a Band-Aid. She looked at it and said, "Well, its not too bad, James. I think we should

YOU

wash it before we bandage it, don't you?" James did not want it washed because he

ACT

thought it would sting. But he was afraid to tell Miss Smith. He just acted brave.

a   *WHEN*

When it was washed and bandaged, he thanked Miss Smith. Then he rushed out to

the playground to show everyone his shiny new bandage.

Passage from Lois A. Bader, *Reader's Passages to accompany Bader Reading and Language Inventory* (3rd ed.), p. 13. Columbus, OH: Merrill/Prentice Hall, 1998. Reprinted with permission.

Appendix G   Diagrams of Expository Text Structures

Cause and Effect

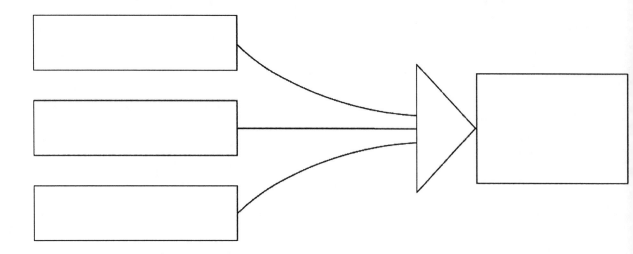

Problem and Solution

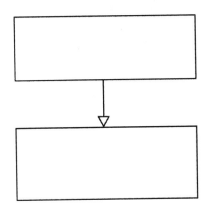

Comparison/Contrast

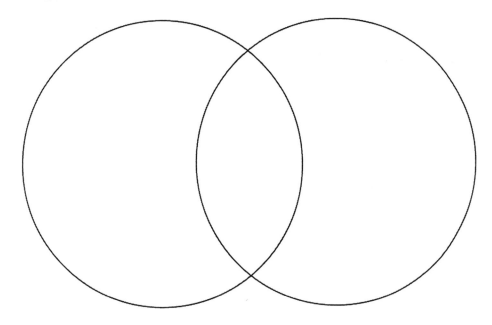

Sequence

1.

2.

3.

4.

5.

Description

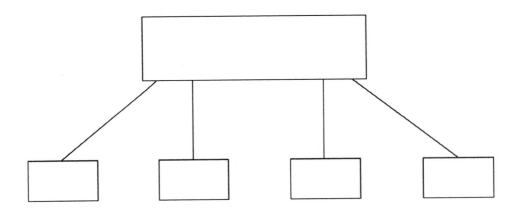